Rhythm of Peace
Cultivating Peace in Daily Life

Volume 1

Deborah L. Aikens, Ph.D.

CRESCENT PUBLISHING
Eugene, Oregon

Rhythm of Peace: Cultivating Peace in Daily Life, Vol. 1
Deborah L. Aikens, Ph.D.

Crescent Publishing
90 E. 27th Avenue, Suite A
Eugene, OR 97405
info@crescent-publishing.com

Acknowledgments of permission to reprint copyrighted materials begin on page 252, which constitutes an extension of this copyright page.

Unattributed quotations are by Deborah L. Aikens.

Publisher's Cataloging-in-Publication
(Provided by Quality Books, Inc.)

      Aikens, Deborah L.
        Rhythm of peace : cultivating peace in daily life /
      Deborah L. Aikens.
        p. cm.
        Includes bibliographical references.
        LCCN 2005926120
        ISBN-13: 978-0-9748500-1-6
        ISBN-10: 0-9748500-1-2

      1. Peace of mind. 2. Peace. 3. Health. I. Title.

      BF637.P3A35 2008   158.1
                    QBI07-60026

Book Production by Eva Long and the *Rhythm of Peace* staff
Cover Design by Tara Kemp, www.kempdesign.com
Cover Photograph by Randall Hodges, www.randalljhodges.com
Printed by Koke Printing, Eugene, Oregon

*Dedicated to
the spirit of peace
and peacemakers throughout the world.*

~

*Positive creativeness
is the fundamental quality of the human spirit.
Let us welcome all those who,
surmounting personal difficulties …
propel their spirits
to the task of Peacebuilding,
thus ensuring a radiant future.*
NICHOLAS ROERICH

Acknowledgments

Many people have generously offered their skills, resources, support, and vision to the process of creating this book and the *rhythm of peace* community website. It is with heartfelt gratitude that I acknowledge family members, friends, partners, and colleagues—each for their unique and valuable contributions:

Mark Aikens, Roni Bernard, Linda Bovard, Michael Chafran, Warren Colvin, Suz Copenhafer, Dana Davis, Ann Devine, Dennis Gallagher, Jason Halstead, Jonathon Hensley, Katherine Hitchcock, Mark Hoy, Sandy Karsten, Lori Keller, Tara Kemp, Eva Long, Jacque Lueth, Patricia Lueth, Patricia Moore, Robert Powell, Julian Pscheid, Cathy Renter, Linda Sattler, Roni Simone, Barb Suter, Renée Taylor, Cathie Walker, and Linda Weaver.

I extend my admiration and deepest appreciation to the entire creative team at Empire Group, Inc. in Portland, Oregon, for generously contributing their artistic, business, and technical skills to the development of the online home for the *rhythm of peace* community.

I offer my appreciation to all the participants in the *rhythm of peace* community for their willingness to make peace a priority in daily life, and for their generous hearts and good will.

Table of Contents

Rhythm of Peace

*a grassroots peace project
dedicated to cultivating peace, renewing health,
and building community*

MISSION

The mission of the *Rhythm of Peace* Project is

*to encourage and inspire
people of all ages and beliefs
to make peace a daily priority,*

*to actively cultivate peace in their homes,
workplaces, and communities, and*

*to promote the values that
build a healthy foundation
for a culture of peace.*

www.rhythmofpeace.org

Introduction

$\mathcal{W}$elcome to the *rhythm of peace* community! We're an informal network of individuals, groups, and organizations that cares about peace. What unites us is our longing for peace and our concern about the future. We agree that it's important to be proactive in cultivating peace in our homes and families, in our workplaces and communities, and in the world at this critical time in history. We recognize the connection between healing ourselves and healing the world around us.

Those who find their way to the *Rhythm of Peace* Project[1] represent a broad range of interests. We care about peace and social justice, economic fairness, civil rights, the environment, human rights, women's rights, and children's rights. We strive to make healthy choices and to live with purpose and meaning. We tend to use alternative and complementary health care practices alongside traditional ones, and value prevention as well as treatment. Collectively, we practice a broad range of spiritual disciplines and seek a healthy relationship with the earth and its

---

[1] *Rhythm of Peace* is a project of the Northwest Center for Health Promotion (NCHP), a non-profit educational organization in Eugene, Oregon. It promotes healthy living as a foundation for peace. For more information visit www.rhythmofpeace.org.

resources. If these values are aligned with your own, we hope you'll join us in our efforts for peace.

Many in our network do not see themselves as activists and are frustrated with the political process. Others have felt isolated and alone because their values are currently not reflected in our mainstream cultural institutions. Individually and collectively, the men and women participating in the *rhythm of peace* community make a sincere effort to cultivate peace in their lives each day. This vitally important grassroots activity is growing, quietly and steadily. It's one of the intentions of this book to support and expand this activity.

Everyone agrees that the need for peace is urgent. We live in turbulent and uncertain times. Those of us who long for peace know it's a daily challenge to shape our thoughts, feelings, and actions toward peace, especially when there are so many forces around us that seem to work against it. We also agree that *now* is the time for people who care about peace to find their voices and take action.

The Rhythm of Peace Project

This book is part of the *Rhythm of Peace* Project—a grassroots effort that encourages people of all ages to make peace a priority in their busy lives. The project addresses three human needs common to people of all cultures and beliefs—the need to *cultivate peace*, the need to *renew health*, and the need to *build community*.

Cultivating peace. In this book you'll find a collection of universal themes geared toward cultivating peace. The themes highlight some of the physical, emotional, mental, social, and spiritual tools we can use to create the conditions for peace in our lives. They encourage a practical balance between cultivating inner peace and cultivating peace in the world around us.

There are 30 themes, one for each day of the month. They can be explored individually, with family or friends, and/or in small group gatherings. They create a support structure for remembering peace each day and taking effective actions for peace each month.

Why a daily focus on peace? Because no matter what else is going on in our lives, peace remains vitally important for all of us. It's important on those days when the world's turmoil is dramatically highlighted in the news or during a crisis. And it's just as important *every* other day, in the midst of our rhythms and routines, our sorrows and celebrations, our victories and challenges.

Renewing health. Creating the conditions where peace can take root and thrive is a complex and long-term challenge. We're all susceptible to the depletion of chronic stress. Sustaining our hope and our ability to act for peace over the long term requires that we take care of our health and renew our resources on a regular basis.

The themes that follow echo the common sense wisdom that the choices we each make about our own health influence the health of our families, our workplaces, and our communities. The themes will encourage you to be proactive in renewing resources, reducing stress, and restoring natural rhythms to build a healthy foundation for peace.

Building community. Each of us who cares about peace is called to action in a unique way. All of our expressions are important. Our combined efforts create a dynamic and healing *rhythm of peace.* As we link our diverse expressions, while retaining our individuality, we create a powerful force for change. We can draw on the support and warmth of a community of like-minded souls stretching across the globe.

How It Works

You're invited to participate in the *rhythm of peace* community by joining in a daily focus on peace. This book offers a simple structure for remembering peace each day and linking with others who also strive to make peace a priority in their busy lives. Each day, we informally join together to reflect on a universal theme related to cultivating peace.

The 30 themes that follow guide us through a calendar month—one cycle of the *rhythm of peace*. After a month, the cycle repeats. Each new cycle builds on the experiences of the last and offers a new opportunity to practice the skills of cultivating peace in our daily activities.

Each monthly cycle has a beginning, middle, and end. As we repeat the themes each month, we establish a stable rhythm. This allows us to observe the changes within and around us as our personal understanding of peace grows and deepens through the months.

Included after each theme are a couple of pages to write your own inspirations, alternative versions of the daily themes or new themes to make the rhythm more personal to your needs and interests. A new cycle of the *rhythm of peace* begins on the first of each month, a natural time to invite friends to join us. With each month we expand our own awareness of peace, and expand the community of people joining in a daily focus.

What does daily participation in the *Rhythm of Peace* Project look like? For some, it means keeping this book on their desk or by their bed, taking note of the theme each morning, and using it as an anchor for cultivating peace and reducing stress during a busy day of activities. For others, the daily theme might be included in a prayer or meditation, or it might generate a discussion about peace with family and co-workers.

Some members of the *rhythm of peace* community meet in small groups once a week or once a month (or through e-mail) to support actions for peace, share challenges, and celebrate results. Others join the daily reflections now and then, as time and circumstances allow. It's easy to start, stop, and begin again by simply turning to the theme associated with the day you'd like to participate (first theme on the first day of the month, second theme on the second day of the month, and so on).

Whatever your level or style of participation, we will have one or more shared intentions such as:

- ↩ a desire for peace, both within our own hearts and in the world,
- ↩ a recognition that our different expressions are important and necessary,
- ↩ a commitment to make peace a priority in daily life,
- ↩ a willingness to act and to sustain our efforts through time,
- ↩ a desire to live healthy, authentic lives.

Rhythm and Healing

Rhythm is at the heart of life. Rhythm *is* life. From deep within our biological processes to the wide spaces embracing the planets in our solar system and beyond, countless rhythms influence every breath and heartbeat. Restoring rhythm is one of the most basic principles of healing.

These are chaotic and unsettling times. Turmoil is increasing for many. The pace of everyday life is fast and getting faster. Dealing with stress in healthy ways continues to be a challenge for all of us. In these conditions, the natural rhythms of healthy living can easily break down, and we live with those consequences every day—personally, nationally, and globally.

The absence of peace is a dramatic reflection of our collective loss of rhythm, a condition that affects us all. Restoring rhythm in our lives influences everything—how we think, how we feel, and the choices we make. When we make healthy choices about how we live, and how we relate to each other, we build a strong foundation for peace.

Inherent in rhythm is wisdom. It takes wisdom to meet our challenges successfully. Frenzied thinking, driven by fatigue, stress, and emotional turmoil, is not potent enough for what we must do. For many of us, the constant tension between the longing for peace and the reality of escalating pressures around us is one of the key challenges of our lives. A daily focus on peace can bring clarity, compassion, and balance to our busy activities. When we link our efforts, we can make a meaningful contribution to a world so in need of peace and healing.

Time

The themes in this book also address time and its many faces. Time can heal or time can harden, depending on how we use it. Rhythms unfold in time and influence our perception of it. When rhythms are in order, time becomes an ally. We have time to do what we need to do, time to think things through, and time to digest what's happening. We enjoy, treasure, even savor time. When there's warmth in the heart, the passage of time is more peaceful. In these moments, time is a gift and we want to use it graciously.

When we've lost our sense of rhythm, when disharmony prevails, time can become an enemy. When we feel that time is against us, we can wage an endless war. One minute we're tired of it and try to "kill" it. In the next minute, we try to slow it down or frantically try to save a little of it, or even steal it, because we're so afraid that it's running out. In still another moment, we could care less about time and waste it.

Sadly, when we waste time, we also waste resources, opportunities, and possibilities. When rhythms are distorted, stress is high and it's common to feel bound to a clock that is moving too fast. Far from friendly, time can then seem like a cruel tyrant.

The themes in this book explore time and rhythm as essential elements in cultivating peace and well-being. Within the themes are invitations to reflect on *this* time in your life (*this* day, *this* month, *this* year). They encourage you to devote some time each day to restoring and maintaining healthy rhythms.

They ask you to reflect on "the times" we're living in—chaotic and uncertain on the one hand, yet full of inspiration and possibility on the other. It's so easy to lose touch with the many rhythms of life—rhythms of the body, of the heart, of the seasons, of the earth.

The themes explore the common challenges of not having enough time and making the best use of time. They invite reflection on individual time (your personal history and future) and humanity's time (our shared history and future), and how they intersect. They address *timing*—good timing and bad timing—when to act and speak, and when to reflect and rest. They invite you to join with others in creating a vibrant *rhythm of peace*, by dedicating some time each day to peace, in a way that has meaning for you.

The Global Voice for Peace

In February 2003, the global community for peace made itself known with unprecedented strength as millions of people in 600 cities around the world raised their voices against war in Iraq. The voice for peace was expressed in many ways—as the longing for peace, the belief in peace, the commitment to peace, and the will to act for peace. This was a worldwide effort to restore some balance in a dramatic situation of escalating disharmony. And every day this effort continues. This dynamic, spirited "voice," to which we each contribute, is reason for hope, as serious questions continue to challenge us:

How do we diversify, sustain, and strengthen the global voice for peace over the long term?

How do we empower people to act and help them to recognize that each healthy action for peace makes a difference?

How do we overcome the isolation, low morale, and intimidation many have experienced as tensions continue to escalate?

How do we cultivate peace in healthy ways so that actions are ethical and effective?

What are the practical tools for cultivating peace every day?

The *rhythm of peace* community is making an effort to address these questions. We're uniting our efforts with the network of peace-minded people throughout the world. This network is growing steadily in response to increasing political, social, financial, and environmental challenges.

Individually and collectively, we represent the will to heal and restore rhythm. Each day more of us connect the longing of our hearts with "right living" and effective actions in the world. We see the results of consciously choosing peace. As we continue to grow, we must believe that our collective voice will become an increasingly powerful force for influencing world events in the weeks and months to come.

Overcoming Isolation and Building Strength

One challenge we all face is to discover how to sustain our efforts for peace through time, for a long time if necessary, and especially during those times when it appears that our efforts are having little impact. In order to do that, we must find ways to dissolve isolation, apathy, and discouragement while fostering collaboration, hope, and consistent action.

We have to learn how to maintain a rhythm of sustained effort in spite of the daily stresses that work against it. And we must find a balance with our personal needs and challenges. Like anything important—loving a child, nurturing a relationship, living with purpose, taking care of our health, learning a skill or an art—daily, rhythmic attention to the task at hand yields more lasting benefits than only paying attention when there's a deadline or a crisis.

A daily focus on peace that is shared by many individuals and groups, each working for peace in their own ways, mobilizes and strengthens the grassroots spirit. We remember *each day* that we're part of a powerful force for peace that is making itself felt around the world. By participating in the *rhythm of peace* community, created by many voices, we're supported and strengthened in our individual efforts. Our experiences of partnership and the warm-hearted spirit of collaboration encourage us to stay active and resilient as we work towards a sustainable peace for all.

The Rhythm of Peace Website
www.rhythmofpeace.org

This book is connected to an educational website, a meeting place for the *rhythm of peace* community. Over the last few years, the Internet has proven its potential to support grassroots dialog. Small groups of people working for peace can now connect easily and purposefully with others around the world.

We hope you'll use the community resources offered on the website. The footnotes in this book will refer you to the website for specific resources that are associated with various themes. Please consider joining the online community so we can keep you up-to-date on the growth and impact of the *rhythm of peace*.

How We Began

The seeds of the *Rhythm of Peace* Project were planted in a meditation group of fifteen men and women in Eugene, Oregon, in the winter of 2003. We've been meeting twice a month for several years exploring themes of healthy living and renewal. In the early months of 2003, we began discussing what we could do together to contribute to peace, and how we might combine our commitments to personal health and self-awareness with social responsibility.

During the months prior to the U.S. invasion of Iraq, the Internet was used effectively as a tool for grassroots organizing. There were many activities offered to bring awareness to the global momentum for peace. One activity was called the "rolling wave." As an example, a national or international peace group would set a specific time for people to join in a prayer, an intention, an action or a moment of silence. The details were communicated by e-mail using the "tell-a-friend" model. People would let others know and then participate at the designated time, in their own time zone. The effect was a rolling wave of commitment to peace that traveled around the world.

Many felt that these events succeeded in connecting people across the globe and supported both collaboration and action. It raised the question for us, "Doesn't it make sense to do something like this *every* day?" We agreed that a daily focus on peace is a healthy way to live. Our conversations and the natural rapport we've developed over the years have provided fertile soil for the *Rhythm of Peace* Project to develop.

We've explored the daily themes together over many months, and gathered feedback on the project through our personal networks. This activity generated the beginning of the *rhythm of peace* community on the West Coast of the U.S. and included participants in Seattle, Washington; Portland and Eugene, Oregon; and San Francisco, Santa Barbara, Los Angeles, and Orange County, California. Our shared desire for peace offers us heart-warming moments, encouragement, and a genuine experience of community and good will. *Will you join us?*

The Time to Act

I believe, as do many of us, that these next few years are critical in our history. The accelerating turmoil calls us to be especially aware of how we're living, and awake to the consequences of our choices and actions. Now is the time to reflect on what's important, to connect with each other, to collaborate, and to act. A key challenge is to refuse to let the frenzied pace of life distort our thinking and relating, and keep us so "wound up" and busy that we lose touch with our natural desire for peace.

My hope is that the following themes support you in discovering and expressing your unique contribution to peace, and that your life is enriched by participating in the *rhythm of peace* community. As you explore the themes for yourself, tailor them to your own needs and interests, and act in ways that have meaning for you, I wish you many moments of genuine peace...

Deborah Aikens
Eugene, Oregon
Fall, 2008

*May we each find the strength and resolve
to express our unique contribution to peace.*

*May we support and encourage each other
along the way.*

*May we discover and celebrate
the true spirit of community.*

*May the path to peace unfold
for us all...*

Vision

Imagine peace.

day 1 ~ *Vision*

Imagine peace.

A new cycle of the *rhythm of peace* begins today, the first day of the month. *A special welcome to new friends who are joining us for the first time!* As we travel through the month together, we'll create new opportunities for peace in our homes, families, and workplaces, and we'll participate in creating a culture of peace for all.

We begin the month by using our imagination to envision peace. In doing so, we both exercise and enliven our creativity. A vision is an inspired picture of the future, a possibility not yet realized. It's born from the fire in the heart, the "yes" to life that urges us to see new vistas of human potential and to reach for our highest ideals. It's our human capacity to begin with a dream and turn it into a living reality. Each one of us can do this.

There's always a natural gap between the present reality and a vision. A vision that is filled with vitality and longing, alive in human hearts, can and will inspire the courage to bridge that gap, no matter how long it might take or how challenging it might be. The energy of the vision influences our thoughts, feelings, and actions each day to move us closer to its realization. As we

day 1 ~ *Vision*

organize our lives around a compelling vision, we discover the power it has to sustain us. And sustain us, it must.

Those who can imagine a world united in peace, and keep that vision alive in their hearts, are a source of hope for everyone. Today is a day to pose questions, imagine, and dream.

What is your vision of personal peace?
How will it look and feel?
What is your vision of world peace?
How will it look and feel?

Consider taking some time to write down your vision of peace, and plan to renew it on the first of each month. Reach for it, and call it forth. Give it your energy and your care. Allow it to grow in vitality and clarity. Bring it to life, and let it guide your actions. *May the hope and the strength of our combined visions surround the world today...*

You must give birth to your images.
They are the future waiting to be born.
Fear not the strangeness you feel.
The future must enter into you long before it happens.

RANIER MARIA RILKE

day 1 ~ Vision

Imagine a World at Peace

Where governments respect the rights
of all their citizens
and settle disputes by the rule of law
for the common good.

Where all people have food, shelter,
and access to medical care,
and children are born into and raised
by healthy families and communities.

Where literacy and education for all
are accomplished facts.

Where economic practices create well being
for all stakeholders,
including communities and the environment.

Where beauty, the arts, and media
inspire the best in people.

Where the benefits of science and technology
enhance all circles of life.

day 1 ~ *Vision*

Where tolerance and appreciation
of diverse religious beliefs are the rule,
spiritual practice is encouraged,
and reverence for life fostered.

Where the earth
in all her natural beauty is treasured
and its resources utilized sustainably,
for this and future generations.

This is a World at PEACE…

You are a Pathway to Peace.
PATHWAYS TO PEACE

~

Tis not too late to seek a newer world.
ALFRED LORD TENNYSON

day 1 ~ *Vision*

(blank ruled lines for writing)

Light tomorrow with today.

ELIZABETH BARRETT BROWNING

day 1 ~ *Vision*

_____

_____

_____

_____

_____

_____

_____

_____

_____

_____

_____

_____

_____

_____

_____

_____

_____

_____

_____

When I dare to be powerful,
to use my strength in the service of my vision,
then it becomes less and less important whether I am afraid.

AUDRE LORDE

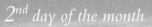

Inner Peace

Cultivate peace within.

day 2 ~ *Inner Peace*

Cultivate peace within.

*M*illions of people around the world express their longing
for peace each day. Many of us recognize that we must start with
ourselves—that peace in individual hearts builds the foundation
for peace in the world. As our inner condition changes, so do we
change the world around us.

The landscape of the inner life is often a battleground for the
warring elements within our own hearts. We all have inner conflicts, contradictory impulses, and confusion. Personal conflicts,
interpersonal conflicts, social, national, and global conflicts are
part of everyday life. Becoming aware of our conflicts helps
to prevent them from erupting and creating consequences we
do not intend.

Today's theme suggests we look inward, tend the inner
landscape, and become aware of what is active within us as
the month begins. We cultivate peace within by taking time
for health-renewing practices such as meditation, relaxation,
contemplation or reflection that increase awareness and nourish
the inner life.

day 2 ~ *Inner Peace*

Through these practices, we discharge the tensions of daily life, relax the body, and approach the peace and stillness that reside in every soul. Guided by the stillness, we deepen our understanding of peace and discover new ways to work with our challenges.

Turning inward allows us to sort out the nature and roots of our conflicts. Some conflicts create only chronic agitation and tension. Others awaken our conscience, sharpen our awareness, and move us to action. Today you might ask:

What are the unnecessary conflicts in my life today that create turmoil, waste energy, and distort my ability to think clearly and act effectively? These conflicts can often be reduced or eliminated through stress reduction practices, exercise, meditation or by making different choices. We can choose to let them go. An example of this type of conflict: chronically complaining about something or someone instead of taking action.

What conflicts in my life urge me to examine my values, my beliefs, and where I stand? These conflicts can lead to growth and understanding, and often need some focused awareness, reflection, and compassion. An example of this type of conflict:

being challenged or criticized by a close family member whose
views on war and peace are different than your own.

*What conflicts call me to action to bring injustice and dishonesty
out into the open?* These conflicts require conscience, energy,
perseverance, and courage. They urge us to create partnerships
and collaborate with others to bring about necessary change. An
example of this type of conflict: social injustice or inequality close
to home or across the world that violates your sense of integrity
and compels you to speak up and take action.

What conflicts are active in your life today?

The many demands of daily life can easily interrupt the
time we might spend cultivating peace within. Yet making this
inner time a priority is good for the soul and helps to reduce
unnecessary turmoil, build reserves for what we need to do, and
calm the restless urgency of modern living. Today's theme is
an invitation to take this time to cultivate peace within, while
keeping in mind that as we each engage in these inner reflections,
we also contribute to peace in the world around us.[2]

---

[2] Use the *Peace Events* calendar at www.rhythmofpeace.org to join with
others in *rhythm of peace* monthly meditations.

day 2 ~ *Inner Peace*

Here's an exercise you might find useful to cultivate inner peace today and throughout the month:

Take a few minutes to sit quietly and identify the inner and outer conflicts in your life today.

Close your eyes, and notice what thoughts and feelings are active. Put your attention on your breathing and take a few deep breaths.

Reflecting on your own traditions and beliefs, connect with what you consider to be a source of peace. For ten to twenty minutes, imagine receiving peace from this source each time you inhale. Let a wave of peace flow through you with each breath. With each exhale, let go of stress, tension, and fatigue. Release the agitation and turmoil that have accumulated from the conflicts in your life.

Relax into the slow rhythm of *inhaling peace, exhaling tension … inhaling peace, exhaling tension … inhaling peace, exhaling tension …* and continue for a few minutes.

When you're ready, open your eyes. As you return to your activities, be willing to see your conflicts with refreshed eyes. Notice what you might want to do differently. Let peace be your guide.

day 2 ~ *Inner Peace*

If there is to be peace in the world,
there must be peace in the nations.

If there is to be peace in the nations,
there must be peace in the cities.

If there is to be peace in the cities,
there must be peace between neighbors.

If there is to be peace between neighbors,
there must be peace in the home.

If there is to be peace in the home,
there must be peace in the heart.

LAO TZU

day 2 ~ *Inner Peace*

World peace must develop from inner peace.

HIS HOLINESS THE DALAI LAMA

day 2 ~ Inner Peace

_____

_____

_____

_____

_____

_____

_____

_____

_____

_____

_____

_____

_____

_____

_____

_____

_____

Looking deeply at our own mind and our own life,
we begin to see what to do and what not to do
to bring about real peace in ourselves and in society.

THICH NHAT HANH

day 2 ~ *Inner Peace*

Who looks outside dreams.
Who looks inside awakens.

C.G. JUNG

Contribution

Honor your contribution to peace.

day 3 ~ *Contribution*

Honor your contribution to peace.

*I*f you're reading this today, it's most likely because you care about peace. And because you care, you have something important to do. Your contribution to peace is unique, and it's personal. It's shaped by your visions and values, and by what's most important to you in life. Today's theme invites you to reflect on your personal contribution to peace, and to recognize the power of linking your efforts with the contributions of others.

As we link our individual efforts for peace, we create a dynamic force for healing and change. We call this force the *rhythm of peace*. It enfolds the many colors, sizes, shapes, and textures of our diverse expressions into an artistic harmony, one that honors each individual contribution while affirming our collective strength. It grows each day as more of us add our voices.

We don't all do the same things, and we don't do the same things in the same ways. Our personal rhythms of activity, involvement, and energy do not rise and fall together. Not everyone is inclined towards politics and activism. Not everyone wants to meditate. We don't all speak the same language, and

day 3 ~ *Contribution*

we don't have the same habits. Some of us have broad outreach extending far beyond our personal circumstances. Others of us express our care in more private ways. We don't need to change this.

Our different expressions can accomplish what needs to be done. These differences need not be occasions for collision. It's the variety of our individual expressions that gives the *rhythm of peace* its power to influence change. Whether each individual effort is judged large or small by outer standards is not important; each genuine expression is necessary and enriches us all.

There is great diversity among the many healthy actions for peace, as these expressions arise from every culture and every faith in the world. Genuine progress towards peace is made every day as we link our own efforts with the efforts of others. We multiply our impact when we support, encourage, and inspire each other to take new and creative actions for peace.

Today's theme affirms our individual efforts as a necessary part of a world symphony—a harmonious sounding of many voices. It's an invitation to honor your unique contribution to peace—wherever you are in the process of discovering and expressing it—and to welcome the contributions of others.

day 3 ~ *Contribution*

Doing so will help you connect to the larger story unfolding in the world, a story in which each of us has a part. As we unite our efforts for peace in the spirit of respect and appreciation, we *will* make progress.[3]

Claim your voice for peace today...
for yourself,
for your family,
for the earth,
for the world.

---

[3] Visit www.rhythmofpeace.org, *Join the Community*, to participate in the *rhythm of peace* online community. You'll receive periodic updates that include community news, resources for cultivating peace, and action alerts.

day 3 ~ *Contribution*

There is a vitality, a life force,
an energy, a quickening that is translated
through you into action.
… this expression is unique.
And if you block it … the world will not have it.
It is not your business to determine how good it is,
nor how valuable,
nor how it compares with other expressions.
It is your business …
to keep the channel open.

MARTHA GRAHAM

day 3 ~ *Contribution*

day 3 ~ *Contribution*

_____

_____

_____

_____

_____

_____

_____

_____

_____

_____

_____

_____

_____

_____

_____

_____

_____

_____

_____

_____

One person, giving all of his or her time to peace,
makes news.
Many people, giving some of their time,
can make history.

PEACE PILGRIM

Priority

Make peace a priority.

day 4 ~ Priority

Make peace a priority.

"I'm too busy!" How often do we say it, think it, and hear it from others? This simple expression is a common explanation for how the most important things in life can get pushed into the background. Once in the background, they can easily disappear into forgetfulness. When we've lost touch with what's most important to us, there is no perspective and definitely no peace.

We all have many demands on our time and energy every day. Some of these demands are genuinely important. Other demands, that seem just as persistent and pressing, may have little or no importance at all. It's these demands that steal time from our true priorities. We have to choose.

Today's theme highlights the way we use time. It's an invitation to exercise the ability to prioritize—to say *yes* to what's really important and *no* to those things that have little genuine value. It's about planning and organizing the day with our highest priorities in mind. Today is a day to refuse to waste time on the unimportant, the trivial, the toxic, and the meaningless—a day to remember who and what really matters.

day 4 ~ *Priority*

One of the intentions of the *Rhythm of Peace* Project is that it be a gentle reminder to remember peace each day. Peace is important to everyone. Its absence is not something to get used to. If we develop the habit of keeping peace in our awareness every day—even if only briefly—we will remember. And because we remember, it will grow in us and influence the way we live.

We live in a world of noise,
yet our conscience is called the "still, small voice."
Unless we heed our own conscience,
we shall continue to be attracted by
what is loud and garish and lose our sense of values.
It is important, therefore, that all of us should determine to set aside
some time each day to commune with ourselves,
to talk with our own still small voice,
to devote even one minute for thoughts of peace ...

U THANT
Secretary General of the United Nations (1961-1971)

day 4 ~ Priority

_____
_____
_____
_____
_____
_____
_____
_____
_____
_____
_____
_____
_____
_____
_____
_____
_____
_____
_____
_____

Things which matter most
must never be at the mercy of things which matter least.
JOHANN WOLFGANG VON GOETHE

Belief

Believe in peace.

day 5 ~ *Belief*

Believe in peace.

*M*ost people want peace. Not everyone who wants peace, however, believes that peace is possible. Beliefs have enormous power to influence our lives, both positively and negatively, and are often hidden from awareness. They shape our perceptions and can severely limit—or profoundly enhance—our potential. As we strive to develop the personal resources to meet the challenges around us, beliefs that support new possibilities, creative solutions, and hope for the future are ever more important.

The capacity to examine beliefs is a natural gift of human intelligence. Today's theme invites us to use clear thinking to explore beliefs about peace, both within ourselves and in the world around us. Negative beliefs constrict vision. It's like we're inside a box. We can't see outside the box but don't know it. The world beyond the box is not available to us, and we live and act as though it doesn't exist.

If we discover negative beliefs, we can change our mind. We can expand our thinking. We can see ourselves, and the world, with awakened eyes. What was once closed to us can open. The change can be dramatic—such is the power of beliefs.

day 5 ~ Belief

Today's theme encourages us to put the power of our thinking behind the desire for peace. Consider one of these questions today:

What are your beliefs about peace?
Can you identify any beliefs that limit your potential for peace?
Have you adopted the belief
that your efforts for peace make a difference?

On what basis might we believe that peace is possible and that our efforts to cultivate peace are meaningful? Here's one view to consider: Human nature is constantly growing and evolving. This can be easily seen from generation to generation. The impulse for growth lives in each one of us. The creative force that causes seeds to grow, and children to dream, and visions to be realized also nourishes the urge for peace.

Life changes. People change. Minds change. Each day is new. Each season is unique. Today it's worth considering the belief that this same creative force makes peace possible.

day 5 ~ Belief

Believing in peace is a choice.
Make that choice today
and the path to peace will unfold before you,
one glorious day at a time.

ANONYMOUS

~

No pessimist ever discovered the secrets of the stars,
or sailed to an uncharted land,
or opened a new heaven to the human spirit.

HELEN KELLER

~

The greatest revolution in our generation
is that of human beings who,
by changing the inner attitudes of their minds,
can change the outer aspects of their lives.

WILLIAM JAMES

day 5 ~ Belief

day 5 ~ *Belief*

_____

_____

_____

_____

_____

_____

_____

_____

_____

_____

_____

_____

_____

_____

_____

_____

_____

_____

_____

_____

*That which dominates our imaginations and our thoughts
will determine our lives and our character.*

RALPH WALDO EMERSON

day 5 ~ Belief

_The negative belief that peace is not possible
is the greatest impediment to achieving peace._

WILLIS HARMON

Prayer

Pray for peace.

day 6 ~ *Prayer*

Pray for peace.

Prayer takes us to the heart of relationship. It originates from a deep desire for connection and intimacy with the source of our faith. Through prayer, we communicate our needs and our gratitude. We express hope that spiritual forces, with wisdom beyond our own, will help guide us to peace. Today, and every day, prayers for peace are being spoken from every corner of the world.

Today's theme acknowledges the value of uniting our prayers for peace.[4] Peace prayers can be found among all the world's religious and spiritual traditions. Through prayer, we affirm a partnership between human longing and divine intent to bring about peace in our hearts and homes, and in the world.

As we each say a prayer for peace today, imagine the strength of our collective prayers reaching around the world. There will be prayers for guidance and protection, prayers for healing and consolation, and prayers that peace and justice be realized on earth. There will be prayers for strength and sustenance and

---

[4] Visit www.rhythmofpeace.org, *Community Center: Pray for Peace*, to read prayers for peace from different traditions.

renewal, and prayers for divine intervention in circumstances
of war, oppression, disaster, and violence. There will be prayers
for peace in marriages and families, and prayers for parents and
children. There will be prayers for nations and governments and
world leaders. As we pray, we link our hearts. This builds the
spiritual foundation of the *rhythm of peace.*

Today we invite intervention, grace, and mercy into our
worldly challenges through our prayers. When we do this
together, our collective prayers communicate our deep desire for
peace and stream upward in unison from around the world.

May we be one world
united in peace.
May peace live in the
hearts of all people.
May our prayers for peace
encircle the earth.
May we each contribute to peace.
May peace light our way.

day 6 ~ Prayer

There is no peace
without the grace of God,
and there is no grace of God
without prayer.

MAHATMA GANDHI

~

Whisper your prayers, recite your prayers,
march your prayers, shout your prayers.
Sing, draw, dance your prayers.
Pray as your heart leads you.

Persevere in your prayers, trust in your prayers,
and have faith in a God who hears your prayers.
In this time of trial,
how can we do less?

JANE VENNARD

day 6 ~ Prayer

day 6 ~ Prayer

day 6 ~ Prayer

_____

May we have peace.
May we be well.
May we be of good will,
today and always.

BUDDHIST PRAYER

Rhythms of Life

Restore the rhythms of healthy living.

day 7 ~ Rhythms of Life

Restore the rhythms of healthy living.

We live in a universe of rhythms. The hectic pace of modern lifestyles tends to disrupt them. Cycles of expansion and contraction, increase and decrease, light and darkness are at work in every aspect of daily life. These are facts of human nature, and acceptance of these rhythms brings us a little closer to peace.

Many of us feel the pressure to accomplish more in less time. It's so easy to *over*eat, *over*do, *over*think, *over*react, and lose touch with the rhythms of healthy living. When the pace of life accelerates, so does chaos. Some thoughtful attention to balancing personal rhythms helps to restore order and well-being.

Throughout a typical day, periods of high activity, energy, and concentration cycle with periods of lower energy and performance. It's easy to observe the highs and lows; we all have them. A mid-morning and a mid-afternoon lull are familiar to most people. These periods of lower energy often signal the need for a short break. We can easily override these signals, and often do. If we do so regularly, however, rhythms break down.

The effects of chronically overriding daily rhythms include the whole range of physical and emotional stress symptoms—

muscle tension, anxiety, confusion, fatigue, poor concentration, and insomnia, to name a few. In the midst of these symptoms, peace is distant and elusive—perhaps forgotten—as the tensions of the moment seem to demand our full attention.

Being aware of the natural rising and falling of energy levels throughout the day helps keep our rhythms intact. If we take a few minutes to relax and stretch when our energy drops, our mind-body system releases stress and fatigue, and prepares for the next period of concentration and activity. To pause in response to the natural movement of a rhythm is not a failure of performance. On the contrary, a few minutes devoted to maintaining healthy rhythms throughout the day often results in being more focused physically, emotionally, and mentally.

Today's theme emphasizes the importance of restoring rhythm in our daily activities. In doing so, we support our health as well as cultivate fertile ground for peace. Today you might identify a personal rhythm that is out of balance and make an effort to restore it throughout the month. *Is there one that immediately comes to mind?* Some common responses include: not enough sleep, too much food, too little exercise, not enough time to reflect, too many commitments or too much noise.

day 7 ~ *Rhythms of Life*

Rhythm renews and rhythm heals. The restoration of one rhythm influences all the others in a complementary way. As we each strive for some harmony in daily life, our collective efforts contribute a healthy vitality and resilience to the *rhythm of peace*.

A suggestion for today: Notice your cycles of energy and concentration throughout the day. Instead of pushing past the low points, take a short break and see if it makes a difference to the quality of your day.

Let us breathe deeply
in the rhythms of life,
of the earth,
of action and rest.
WAYNE MULLER

day 7 ~ Rhythms of Life

When anxious, uneasy and bad thoughts come,
I go to the sea,
and the sea drowns them out
with its great wide sounds,
cleanses me with its noise,
and imposes a rhythm
upon everything in me
that is bewildered and confused.

RAINER MARIA RILKE

~

The bewildering hurly-burly of life,
the pressure imposed by forces outside ourselves,
ever threaten to smother our natural cycles.
We have lost our natural sense of rhythm, our sense of timing.
We do not know when to ebb and when to flow!

WILLIAM BRYANT

day 7 ~ *Rhythms of Life*

day 7 ~ *Rhythms of Life*

Tension is who you think you should be.
Relaxation is who you are.

CHINESE PROVERB

Action

Take action for peace.

day 8 ~ Action

Take action for peace.

*T*oday's theme focuses on action—direct, specific action. Each one of us is in the process of discovering, shaping, expressing, and living our unique contribution to peace. Wherever we are in that process, there's always a meaningful next step.

Past experiences. Current skills and interests. Desire and will. Today's circumstances and tomorrow's commitments. World events. Time, energy, and resources. Passion and spirit. These are some of the many factors that influence what we choose to do this month for peace. Our actions will also be shaped by the failures, hardships, and personal weaknesses that challenge us, as these experiences teach humility and season maturity.

When the full range of our human experience is acknowledged, our actions become more *authentic*—genuine, real, and from the heart—rather than determined by empty "shoulds," rigid standards or the expectations of others. We act from the earthiness of our life experiences as well as from the inspirations and visions that live through us—embracing both our light and our darkness. Taking potent actions for peace, both within ourselves and in the world, calls us to be authentic, original, and profoundly human.

day 8 ~ *Action*

The healing potential of the *rhythm of peace* is based on trust—trust that each person called to act for peace will find his or her own right actions, and trust that our combined actions will one day bring a tangible and lasting harmony to the world. With a daily focus on peace, our actions will evolve and change each month as we deepen our authenticity and take into account the individual demands of our lives and world events as they unfold. Today's theme encourages authentic actions for peace.

What will you do this month that is authentic for you?
What actions will contribute to peace while taking into consideration your time and talents, your resources, and the other necessities of your life?

Your actions for peace this month may be personal, local, national or global. Your efforts may extend deep into your inner life or reach far across the world or both. They may be focused on an individual, a family, a group, an organization, a community, a movement or a government. You may decide to give time, money, care, ideas or support. Reflect on your actions for peace this month. From deep within your heart, *what are you called to do?*[5]

---

[5] Visit www.rhythmofpeace.org, *Community Center: Take Action for Peace*, for suggestions on actions you might take for peace this month.

day 8 ~ *Action*

Moral excellence comes about as a result of habit.
We become just by doing just acts,
temperate by doing temperate acts,
brave by doing brave acts.

ARISTOTLE

~

Nobody made a greater mistake
than he who did nothing
because he could do only a little.

EDMUND BURKE

~

I am only one,
but still I am one.
I cannot do everything,
but still I can do something;
and because I cannot do everything
I will not refuse to do the something that I can do.

EDWARD EVERETT HALE

day 8 ~ *Action*

I long to accomplish great and noble tasks,
but it is my chief duty to accomplish humble tasks
as though they were great and noble.

HELEN KELLER

day 8 ~ *Action*

Almost anything you do will seem insignificant,
but it is very important that you do it.

MAHATMA GANDHI

day 8 ~ *Action*

A vision without a task is but a dream.
A task without a vision is drudgery.
A task with a vision is the hope of the world.

ANONYMOUS

Conscience is the chamber of justice.
ORIGEN

Conscience

Let wisdom be your guide.

day 9 ~ *Conscience*

Let wisdom be your guide.

When we take action on something that's important to us, we want a good outcome. We want our actions to make a difference. Even when we make an effort to consider the impact and the consequences, sometimes we do things that don't turn out at all the way we intended. Sometimes our actions are guided by thinking that is distorted or even completely inaccurate, costing us valuable time, resources, and well-being. How can we make our actions for peace most effective?

Today's theme highlights the value of turning inward to seek wisdom before we act. *What to do, how to do it, with whom, and when?* These are questions that cannot be answered by reason alone. Turning inward to the light of conscience brings integrity to our actions, and helps us choose actions and timing that will be most effective. You know that old expression, "When it's right and when it's true, a little goes a long way."

When was the last time you or someone around you did just the right thing, at just the right moment, in a way that made a real and tangible impact? Often these are memorable, heart-warming, even grace-filled moments—when clear, well-timed actions connect needs with results. These are actions that inspire and heal.

Let's pause today, before each important action we take, to invite wisdom to illumine and influence it. Imagine the results if all the actions taken today in the name of peace were guided by wisdom. By the end of the day we would have a different world. Actions, guided by conscience, give the *rhythm of peace* its integrity and a potency that only wisdom can provide.

> *One single act of generosity,*
> *thoughtfully chosen,*
> *respectfully timed,*
> *can change a life.*
> *Watch for the ripe moment*
> *and act.*

~

> *When will our consciences*
> *grow so tender*
> *that we will act to prevent human misery*
> *rather than avenge it?*
> ELEANOR ROOSEVELT

day 9 ~ *Conscience*

_____

_____

_____

_____

_____

_____

_____

_____

_____

_____

_____

_____

_____

_____

_____

_____

*Labor to keep alive
that little spark of celestial fire,
called conscience.*

GEORGE WASHINGTON

day 9 ~ *Conscience*

_____

_____

_____

_____

_____

_____

_____

_____

_____

_____

_____

_____

_____

_____

_____

_____

Nothing is more powerful
than an individual acting out of his conscience,
thus helping to bring the collective conscience to life.

NORMAN COUSINS

Balance

Balance care of self with care of others.

day 10 ~ *Balance*

Balance care of self with care of others.

*C*an we take care of our personal needs and address the needs of the world at the same time? One answer is that we can, because we must. But we need to meet this challenge in a way that makes sense—we have to stay *healthy*, we have to stay *awake*, and we have to stay *involved*.

When we find ourselves aligned with the mission of peace, there's a natural desire to act. This raises many questions, such as:

> *What specific needs will I address?*
> *Where will I focus my actions?*
> *Will I be effective?*
> *What time, skills, and resources will I contribute?*

Everyone has needs. Our families, schools, workplaces, and communities have needs. Millions of individuals and families in our own country, and across the world, have genuine needs at a level we can barely imagine. Finding a healthy balance between attending to our personal needs and attending to the needs of others, including those on distant shores, presents a fundamental life challenge for everyone.

day 10 ~ Balance

Too much focus on personal circumstances can leave us self-absorbed, isolated, and unrelated to the world. Too much focus on the needs of others can leave us exhausted, prone to resentment and despair, and without the necessary clarity of mind and heart to make sound choices. Neither of these conditions is good for anyone.

Today's theme encourages using both compassion and common sense to address the challenge of balancing personal needs with the needs of others. This balance is never static, and always changing. We approach it but never reach it, making adjustments every day. With a strong commitment to self-care, and sensitivity to the needs of others, we're better able to discern where to focus our actions.

Sustaining our participation in activities that cultivate peace is a complex and long-term challenge. It takes time and energy, courage and resilience. It takes commitment. The challenges of creating a culture of peace should never be underestimated. Yet, we can be certain that those of us who are inspired by the vision of *one human family, united in peace*, will meet the challenge, and we will do so with every resource we have.

day 10 ~ Balance

At the most fundamental level, genuine self-care recognizes the needs of body, soul, and spirit. It helps clear the mind, soften the heart, and generate fruitful actions. We each find a personal blend of a diet that works for us, exercise we're willing to do, stress reduction and renewal practices that sustain us, spiritual practices that bring us connection and meaning, support from others, etc.

Our self-care doesn't have to be perfect. We do what we can. This care we give ourselves provides us with the energy and clarity required to meet our personal needs while participating in addressing the needs of the world. Far from being selfish, it builds stability and strength, and enriches our capacity to engage with life and give generously. Today is a good day to reflect on the balance between your personal self-care *and* your engagement with the needs of the world.

We'll continue to strive for a healthy balance between care of self and care of others in the months and years ahead. This will give us the energy for what we need to do. May all who contribute to the *rhythm of peace*, and have the courage to take action, be nourished and sustained in their efforts.

day 10 ~ Balance

The time for contemplation is the spring that feeds our action,
and our action will be as deep as the spring.
We need time to allow the spirit to clear the obstacles
—the clinging debris and mud—
that keeps the spring from flowing freely
from its clear, deep source.
And we need time for the spring to overflow
into insightful, compassionate action.

THOMAS MERTON

~

To have a firm persuasion in our work—
to feel that what we do is right for ourselves
and good for the world at the same time—
is one of the great triumphs of human existence.

DAVID WHYTE

day 10 ~ Balance

day 10 ~ Balance

... the health of the human psyche
and the health of the world
are inextricably related,
and we cannot truly heal one
without healing the other.
GAIL STRAUB

Legacy

Leave the world a better place.

day 11 ~ *Legacy*

Leave the world a better place.

$\mathcal{T}$he desire to leave a better world for our children, and for future generations, is natural for all people who strive for peace. This desire extends our actions far into the future. It gives meaning to actions we take now that may not bear fruit for a long time. We may not see all the effects of what we do, but we can trust that others will benefit. Someone whose face we will never see, or name we will never know, will be encouraged and sustained by the actions we take today.

Fulfilling the need to leave a positive legacy—to know without a doubt that our efforts and choices contribute to others— is fundamental to living a healthy life. Today's theme invites you to reflect on your personal legacy. Do those closest to you know where you stand about peace and what you're doing about it? Do they know why it's important to you?

What we do to cultivate peace this month becomes part of the current of life that flows unceasingly from the past to the future. This perspective helps to overcome frustration and discouragement when, in the face of current world tensions, we may wonder if our actions are making much impact. It puts

day 11 ~ *Legacy*

our personal challenges in a larger context, one that connects us both to our ancestors and to the generations of the future. Each generation will carry the flame of peace for its time, and then pass it on. *Our time is now.*

Today we affirm that our actions help realize the visions of those who have lived before us. We can appreciate all of our efforts, even the little things, and recognize that what we do now prepares the soil in which the visions of the world's children will thrive. Future generations will sustain the *rhythm of peace* in new ways, appropriate to their times.

Today we remember the river of life in which we all live. We can feel confident that this continuous current will carry our good will far into the future, and trust that none of our efforts will be lost. *May we each do our part* to ensure a healthy future.

What you leave behind
is not what is engraved in stone monuments,
but what is woven into the lives of others.

PERICLES

day 11 ~ *Legacy*

I believe we are reaching
a unique point in our evolution where
we can make a promise
to future generations.
It is a declaration that
we will not forget them
in the rush and busyness of our day-to-day lives.
The promise is our marriage
with the larger flow of life
—both past and future—
and our recognition that
we are now a critical link
in maintaining the integrity of that flow.
It is our sacred covenant with the future
whereby we send ahead
not only our good intentions,
but also our commitment of active engagement
to turn the direction of our evolution
in favor of a promising future.

DUANE ELGIN

day 11 ~ Legacy

You have as yet no faces we can see,
no names we can say.
But we need only hold you in our mind,
and you teach us patience.
You attune us to measures of time
where healing can happen,
where soil and souls can mend.
You reveal courage within us we had not suspected,
love we had not owned.

JOANNA MACY

day 11 ~ Legacy

day 11 ~ *Legacy*

Memories of our lives,
of our works and our deeds,
will continue in others.

Rosa Parks

Hidden Charity

Cultivate peace with love.

day 12 ~ Hidden Charity

Cultivate peace with love.

The events in today's news will no doubt be a topic of conversation for many. But they will only tell a piece of the human story, and often not the best piece, to be sure. There's another story to be told, one just as significant as any news we'll ever hear. It's a story of human nature at its best—the millions of gestures of love and good will expressed throughout every moment of every day, around the clock, and across the world.

These expressions of love may not be dramatic, sensational or "newsworthy" by current standards. In fact, many of them occur without anyone ever knowing—a silent prayer, an anonymous gift, the removal of garbage from a forest trail, a moment of forgiveness, the silencing of a criticism, an extra effort to lighten the load of another...

These invisible acts of love are not colored by the need for credit or acknowledgment. They're not part of a bargain, "I'll love you, if you'll love me." They're not a strategy to "look good" or win favor. On the contrary, they're genuine expressions of the human heart at its best, quietly and steadily transforming chaos and hardship.

day 12 ~ Hidden Charity

These quiet gifts of hidden charity bring warmth to the
rhythm of peace. Today's theme suggests we pause and remember
this story. Why? Because it's a true story, and because it's
important to have a balance to the other news we hear. And
because the *collective force* of millions of gestures of love is
enormous. Awareness of this force awakens our vision, and we
can see it working everywhere. We only have to look. *May we
each participate in this story today*. It may be the best news of
the day.

> *If we want there to be peace in the world,*
> *we have to be brave enough*
> *to soften what is rigid in our hearts,*
> *to find the soft spot and stay with it.*
> *We have to have that kind of courage*
> *and take that kind of responsibility.*
> *That's the true practice of peace.*
> PEMA CHÖDRÖN

~

> *The little unremembered acts of kindness and love*
> *are the best parts of a person's life.*
> WILLIAM WORDSWORTH

day 12 ~ Hidden Charity

_____
_____
_____
_____
_____
_____
_____
_____
_____
_____
_____
_____
_____
_____
_____
_____
_____
_____

Peace is a daily, a weekly, a monthly process,
gradually changing opinions,
slowly eroding old barriers,
quietly building new structures.

JOHN F. KENNEDY

day 12 ~ Hidden Charity

Few of us can do great things,
but all of us can do small things
with great love.

MOTHER TERESA

Humility

Pause before you judge.

day 13 ~ *Humility*

Pause before you judge.

"What's in it for *me*?" "I want it *my* way!" These familiar phrases reflect the drive to promote a personal agenda. When this drive is carried out aggressively, and at the expense of others, it can be disastrous to peace.

Humility is one of the true gifts of life. It's a natural companion to peace. Rather than assuming that we're right or wrong, which is so characteristic of pride, humility allows us to experience life without the bias of a self-serving lens. It helps us temper the ever-present human tendency to judge and criticize, inevitably creating walls and wars.

Today's theme is about cultivating humility in our inter-actions with others. It's about refusing the temptation to feel superior or inferior to anyone. By doing so, we quiet the inner dialog that relentlessly assesses the virtues and values of others, and draws conclusions without all the facts. We can make the choice to sacrifice those things we might say that fall into the category of gossip, mean-spirited opinions, and unnecessary criticism—the common battles of daily life.

day 13 ~ Humility

These negative expressions arise in moments when emotional turmoil and the urge to be right are stronger than the hunger for peace. It's easy to forget. The drive for power is part of human nature. We can see the consequences of it many times every day in our personal interactions as well as in world events. It remains one of the greatest challenges to a sustainable peace. Not one of us is exempt from this challenge. How we deal with it, in ourselves and in others, is one of the key themes of our times. History will record the outcome of our choices.

The cultivation of humility supports us in embracing diversity, so important to the health of the *rhythm of peace*. We strive to seek solutions that build relationships and refuse actions that destroy them. Humility helps us make necessary course corrections when we need to, instead of stubbornly defending positions and actions that are not working. It leaves us open to discovering new and fruitful solutions to the conflicts we have with each other. With humility, we pause before we judge, and in that pause lives a world of possibilities.

We come nearest to the great,
when we are great in humility.
RABINDRANATH TAGORE

day 13 ~ *Humility*

The antidote for the poison of pride
is humility—
the humility to realize
that we're not an island,
that the quality of our lives
is inseparably connected
to the quality of the lives of others,
that meaning is not in
consuming and competing,
but in contributing.
We are not laws unto ourselves,
and the more we begin to value
principles and people,
the greater will be our peace.

STEPHEN COVEY

day 13 ~ Humility

day 13 ~ *Humility*

_____
_____
_____
_____
_____
_____
_____
_____
_____
_____
_____
_____
_____
_____
_____
_____
_____
_____
_____
_____

We look forward to the time
when the power of love
will replace the love of power.
Then will our world
know the blessings of peace.

WILLIAM E. GLADSTONE

day 13 ~ *Humility*

Help me not to despise or oppose
what I do not understand.

WILLIAM PENN

There is a life pouring into this world,
and it pours from an inexhaustible source.

JOSEPH CAMPBELL

Renewal

Renew your resources.

day 14 ~ Renewal

Renew your resources.

*T*he wheel of life turns round and round. Sometimes the repetition can be exhausting. It can leave us feeling empty, used up, and worn out. The need for cyclic renewal—to be refreshed and regenerated by vibrant life forces—is basic to all of life, yet few people get enough genuine renewal these days. For many people, time "off" is used to catch up on chores and errands, and serves the mission of "getting things done." It's not easy to stop when there's so much to do.

Everything we do takes energy. We draw on physical, emotional, social, mental, and spiritual reserves of energy every day. Renewing these resources is a cornerstone of health. Without sufficient renewal, we're forced to draw on our emergency reserves to fulfill daily tasks. When this becomes a habit, it creates the condition of chronic stress and leads to a depleted state of body, soul, and spirit. Certainly, in this condition, we're not at our best. Unfortunately, in our culture, this condition has become normalized.

Renewal gives us a little time off the wheel. We sense when our reserves are low, and then intentionally take some time to

day 14 ~ Renewal

replenish them. How we use that time is personal to our own needs and interests. What's renewing for one might be just "one more thing to do" for another. We can receive life-giving, restorative energy through music, art, movement, meditation, prayer, poetry, nature, solitude, service, communication— anything that we find genuinely engaging and refreshing. Sometimes, we just need a good rest or a little free time.

Today's theme honors the need for cyclic renewal, and invites us to explore its many benefits. Renewal gives us a chance to exhale and regain perspective. We temporarily disconnect from our preoccupation with the clock. We sort, prioritize, and generally clean the inner house.

In the time we dedicate to renewal, we realign with an inner compass that guides and directs our next steps. We open our minds and hearts, and the circumstances of our lives, to new and fresh impulses. *We are made new again.*

In an era when we're expected to get as much done as possible, the need for renewal can be perceived as a sign of weakness or self-indulgence. Worse, it can be viewed as time wasted because it's judged as unproductive. This is a condition that must be opposed, as it has become a tragic disorder of social life.

day 14 ~ Renewal

Without sufficient renewal, rhythms easily degenerate into dull, lifeless routines. Life gets flat and loses its color. Stress escalates and energy is lost. Thinking is easily distorted. Passivity, fatigue, and apathy interrupt creative responses to our challenges.

With renewal, it's not so much what we do, but how and when we do it—the quality of our attention and the timing. We choose activities that enrich and refresh. We intentionally open ourselves to the vibrant life forces all around us, and allow this energy to flow through us like waves, restoring our reserves and cleansing fatigue and stress. We relax … and find the peace of the moment.[6]

What will you do today to renew your resources?
What is the most important thing you can do
to renew your resources this month?

As we each honor the need for cyclic renewal, we bring fresh energy into our lives and new vitality to the *rhythm of peace*.

---

[6] The *Rhythm of Peace* Project promotes healthy living as a foundation for peace. Visit www.rhythmofpeace.org, *Healthy Living Center*, for stress reduction tools and resources.

day 14 ~ Renewal

We spend most of our time and energy
in a kind of horizontal thinking.
We move along the surface of things …
[but] there are times when we stop.
We sit still.
We lose ourselves in a pile of leaves or its memory.
We listen, and breezes from a whole other world begin to whisper.

JAMES CARROLL

~

When we are truly centered
in the life current flowing through us,
we tend to act in ways that promote
the well-being and harmony of the whole.

DUANE ELGIN

~

The human spirit is naturally generous;
the instant we are filled,
our first impulse is to be useful, to be kind,
to give something away.

WAYNE MULLER

day 14 ~ Renewal

_____
_____
_____
_____
_____
_____
_____
_____
_____
_____
_____
_____
_____
_____
_____
_____
_____
_____
_____
_____
_____

Renewal awakens
those quiet forces within
that refresh, nourish, and sustain
the life we choose to live.

day 14 ~ *Renewal*

*We must always change, renew,
rejuvenate ourselves;
otherwise we harden.*

JOHANN WOLFGANG VON GOETHE

Waxing & Waning

Follow your personal rhythm of peace.

day 15 ~ Waxing & Waning

Follow your personal rhythm of peace.

*I*t's the middle of this month's cycle of the *rhythm of peace—* a good time to pause.

Each of our various interests has a rhythm. There are periods of intense activity and participation that cycle with times of disengagement and pulling back. So it is with peace. Influenced by personal circumstances, as well as by what's going on in the world, our involvement in cultivating peace ebbs and flows. Sometimes energy and participation are high. At other times, attention is focused elsewhere.

One of the objectives of the *Rhythm of Peace* Project is to support individuals and groups in sustaining their efforts for peace over the long term. To be successful in this requires an acceptance of the natural waxing and waning of interest and engagement in all our activities.

The value of uniting our efforts with others who care about peace is that we won't all be waxing or waning at the same time. Some of us are very active and enthusiastic in our efforts to cultivate peace this month. Some are more focused on other important life interests and challenges. Such is the nature of cycles.

day 15 ~ *Waxing & Waning*

There's room in the commitment to peace for the rising and falling tides of energy and momentum. This is natural. We don't need to sustain our commitment to peace at the same level every day. By linking our efforts, the *rhythm of peace* remains strong and steady for all.

Today's theme invites a reflection on your own rhythm of cultivating peace in your life. *Is it waxing or waning?*

If your focus on peace is waning today, stay connected with others. Let the *rhythm of peace* support you for awhile. Its influence will help you keep peace alive in your awareness while you're focused on other things.

If your momentum for peace is strong and you're very active this month, you're contributing to the vitality and stability of the *rhythm of peace* for everyone. Your enthusiasm will encourage and inspire others, and your efforts are sincerely appreciated.

The tides will change from month to month for each of us. This we can accept with compassion. Peace will gradually grow in our lives as we allow our efforts to ebb and flow with everything else that's important to us. This way, peace finds a natural home in daily life and gently influences everything we do.

day 15 ~ Waxing & Waning

All too often, change comes uninvited to
throw our peace and certainty
into doubt and confusion.
The natural order decrees that there be intervals
of vitality and creativity
and intervals of withdrawal and suffering.
But there is no reason to suppose
that such cycles of increase and decrease
deprive our lives of meaning and purpose.
Today, as never before, the world scatters
our inner force in all directions ...
Today, as never before,
we are compelled to rely on
our own sense of destiny ...
we must follow our own path
by the light of our own consciousness
and interior wisdom.

WILLIAM BRYANT

day 15 ~ *Waxing & Waning*

Happiness is not a matter of intensity
but of balance, order, rhythm, and harmony.

THOMAS MERTON

day 15 ~ Waxing & Waning

*Your rhythms are the
melodies of your soul.*

day 15 ~ *Waxing & Waning*

Rhythm is the basis of life,
not steady forward progress.

KABBALAH

Give me the gift of a listening heart.

SOLOMON

Deep Listening

Practice the language of peace.

day 16 ~ Deep Listening

Practice the language of peace.

"You're not listening to me!!" It's heard so often at dinner tables, in bedrooms, classrooms, and workplaces—all the places we try to express ourselves to the people closest to us. For many, it's a silent scream that's never expressed for fear of consequences.

Who doesn't long to be understood? Nobody likes to be rejected, diminished or criticized. To be analyzed, ignored or "fixed" isn't much better. Yet so often, by habit, speaking and listening become weapons in our relationships. It's so common to listen to the voice in our minds about how we'll respond or how we'll defend our position instead of hearing what another is really saying.

How refreshing it is to be listened to with a quiet appreciation for what we're trying to express. This is deep listening. It's more than hearing with the ears, and it's not a technique. People express so much more than can be heard with ears alone.

In deep listening, we strive to open our heart to the one who is speaking. We listen for the feelings, meaning, needs, and longings that might not be obvious in the words. It doesn't require that we agree with what we're hearing, but it does ask that we make a genuine effort to understand another's needs and perceptions. This is today's theme—to listen without fixing or advising or evaluating, and to experience how deep listening cultivates peace.

Learning to speak and listen in ways that encourage peace—practicing the language of non-violence—is a challenge for everyone. Our ability to effectively communicate comes from the recognition that the well-being of others is deeply linked to our own. Through our collective attention to deep listening today, by practicing it and by asking for it, we foster peace in our relationships. Our willingness to listen brings the wisdom of healthy communication to the *rhythm of peace*.[7]

> *Deep listening is miraculous for both listener and speaker.*
> *When someone receives us with open-hearted,*
> *non-judging, intensely interested listening,*
> *our spirits expand.*
>
> SUE PATTON THOELE

---

[7] The *Rhythm of Peace* Project encourages developing communication skills that foster peace. Visit www.rhythmofpeace.org, *Community Center: Communicate for Peace*, for resources.

day 16 ~ *Deep Listening*

_____

_____

_____

_____

_____

_____

_____

_____

_____

_____

_____

_____

_____

_____

_____

_____

_____

_____

_____

_____

_____

_____

Most people do not listen with the intent to understand;
they listen with the intent to reply.

STEPHEN COVEY

day 16 ~ Deep Listening

*There is more hunger
for love and appreciation in this world
than for bread.*

MOTHER TERESA

Help from Above

Receive guidance and inspiration.

day 17 ~ *Help from Above*

Receive guidance and inspiration.

We're not alone in our efforts to cultivate peace in our lives, but there are those difficult times when it would seem so. Sometimes the path is steep, and we feel very alone. During those times, we carry the weight of life with little ease or humor. Today's theme acknowledges turmoil, challenge, and hardship with compassion. It's an invitation to devote this day to awakening, renewing, and deepening our faith.

The wisdom traditions of the world remind us of the abundant resources that continually flow to us from other realms— realms that are beyond the ones we see with our ordinary senses. Guidance and inspiration are continuously offered to help us meet the challenges of life—our individual challenges as well as the national and global challenges we all share.

We each discover our own path to peace. We each shape our own relationship with the source of our faith. Today we can turn our attention to this source with a willingness to receive help in meeting the challenges before us.

Through participating in the *rhythm of peace,* we contribute to building a support structure of trust and good will for all of us. We can look to each other for a sense of connection and belonging while we go about our individual tasks. As we turn our eyes upwards together, we can also count on help from above. We can be certain that help is available to everyone, and no one is excluded.

Today's theme suggests that we maintain an awareness of this support in all of the day's events. One way is to imagine energy streaming towards us from above, like rays of sunlight. We can seek guidance about our needs and challenges, including those things about which we have the most fear and concern. You might ask yourself:

What do I genuinely need this month?
What is my greatest challenge?
What is my deepest concern?

We can use our capacity for deep listening, this time turning our attention upward. If we can affirm that each of us will receive meaningful guidance today, together we will call forth great healing resources into our personal challenges and into the world around us.

day 17 ~ *Help from Above*

To the starry heavens above
I direct my gaze.
Starlight penetrates into my heart ...
Peace streams into my soul.

RUDOLF STEINER
translated by ROBERT POWELL

~

God of life, there are days when the burdens we carry
chafe our shoulders and wear us down;
when the road seems dreary and endless,
the skies gray and threatening;
when our lives have no music in them
and our hearts are lonely,
and our souls have lost their courage.
Flood the path with light, we beseech you;
turn our eyes to where the skies are full of promise.

SAINT AUGUSTINE

day 17 ~ Help from Above

day 17 ~ *Help from Above*

day 17 ~ *Help from Above*

May our thoughts be illumined,
our hearts warmed,
and our actions inspired
by the ever watchful spirit of peace.

The echoes of blessing
can be heard
for a lifetime.

Blessing

Be an instrument of peace.

day 18 ~ *Blessing*

Be an instrument of peace.

A blessing is a natural expression of love. It's a gift, given freely to enrich another. Through blessing we extend to each other our deepest wishes that life bestow its abundant grace. We give and receive blessings at celebrations and special occasions, during times of challenge and hardship, and as part of daily rituals such as the blessing before the evening meal.

In the act of blessing, we invoke the sacred dimension of life. We align with forces greater than ourselves to carry our good will to another. By practicing the art of blessing, we become more attuned to the invisible network that links us together. We can feel that something tangible passes from spirit to spirit and heart to heart. In the atmosphere of blessing, hope is restored and the world makes more sense. The hard edges of living are softened, and judgment is replaced with gratitude.

A blessing might be expressed in a physical way, such as a gift of food, money or shelter. It might be a gift of comfort, reassurance, appreciation or encouragement. It might take the form of offering an opportunity or sharing an insight. Or it might be a prayer, thoughtfully chosen.

day 18 ~ Blessing

A blessing might include spending time with another or it might take almost no time at all. It could be a kind thought, a meaningful word, a loving glance or a simple touch. When a blessing truly carries our good will, energized by our genuine concern for the well-being of another, it becomes a potent instrument of peace.

Most of us are in situations every day that call for blessing. These are circumstances that have become infected with judgment, criticism, cynicism, and conflict. There may be circumstances where anger has erupted into hatred and violence or where hardship has created deep and profound suffering.

What situation in your life is most in need of
a blessing for peace today?
Who will be the recipient of your good will?

Today's theme encourages generosity in these situations and asks us to respond with a well-chosen blessing for peace. By doing so, we bring the healing potential of the *rhythm of peace* into situations where it's most needed. Influence your world today by offering a blessing for peace.

day 18 ~ Blessing

We look to the universe, to the world around us,
to each other, and if we are believers,
to the invisible world of the sacred,
and if we have one basic desire
—voiced or not, recognized or not—
it is that all these things be on our side.
We want life to be our ally:
helping us, empowering us,
enabling us to be safe and happy.
We want good things to come our way:
our wounds healed, our loneliness banished,
our power restored, our fears allayed.
We want alienation to be replaced with belonging,
impoverishment with abundance,
bondage with liberation,
darkness with light.
We want to be blessed.
And in our better moments,
we want to be a blessing for others.

DAVID SPANGLER

day 18 ~ *Blessing*

day 18 ~ Blessing

Do not wait to enjoy the harvest of your life;
you are already blessed.

Wayne Muller

day 18 ~ *Blessing*

Blessing is easiest when it's simply
the overflow from a joyous heart.
But it's when we are able to make the choice to bless
even though everything in us wants to curse and strike out
that we demonstrate the power of the human soul
to choose what builds life and creates wholeness.

DAVID SPANGLER

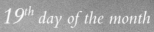

Silence

Find peace in silence.

day 19 ~ *Silence*

Find peace in silence.

*S*pacious. *Deep. Safe. Penetrating. Audible. Refreshing. A sanctuary in time.* These are some of the expressions that describe the rich textures of silence. In silence, we can hear ourselves think and attune our senses to the sounds of peace.

The world is noisy. The noise can be both toxic and intoxicating at the same time. In one moment we might long for peace and quiet. In the next, we might surround ourselves with sounds that mask some inner or outer turmoil we'd rather not feel.

In silence we get reacquainted with ourselves. We turn down the volume of daily life and become aware of quieter voices that live within. Silence cleanses perceptions and heightens awareness, helping us discern the essential from the trivial. We see and hear things that we hadn't noticed before. The waves of the *rhythm of peace* continually flow through our lives; in silence we're more able to experience them.

We can approach silence by reducing unnecessary noise. A period of relaxation or meditation devoted to exploring silence can calm a noisy, congested mind. A silent walk and a light meal

day 19 ~ *Silence*

can soothe a body wound too tight from the day's demands, relaxing the muscles and the nerves. An intentional period without speaking heightens the ability to listen and observe, while offering a rest from social conversation.

It's so common to feel an anxious inner demand to do too much in too little time, compromising both quality and common sense. Silencing this demand restores balance and well-being. Turning off the sounds of technology for an evening allows us to remember what "quiet" feels like. Silently gazing into the night sky reminds us of wider horizons and a sense of purpose.

In exploring silence, we open to deep wells of restorative energy, building our resilience to daily stress. Our collective reflections can help soothe and calm a noisy, chaotic world. *May each of us find the peace in silence today.*

> *May we all grow in grace and peace,*
> *and not neglect the silence that is printed*
> *in the centre of our being.*
> *It will not fail us.*
> THOMAS MERTON

day 19 ~ *Silence*

*In the attitude of silence
the soul finds the path in a clearer light,
and what is elusive and deceptive
resolves itself into crystal clearness.*

MAHATMA GANDHI

day 19 ~ *Silence*

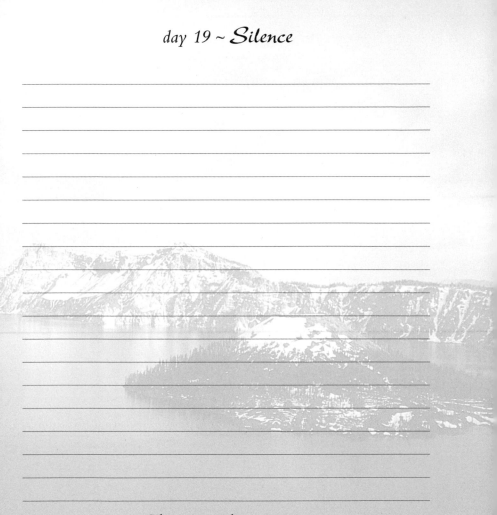

Silence is our deepest nature,
our home,
our common ground,
our peace.
GUNILLA NORRIS

Nature does not hurry,
yet everything is accomplished.

LAO TZU

Natural Laws

Cultivate peace with common sense.

day 20 ~ *Natural Laws*

Cultivate peace with common sense.

 $\mathcal{T}$ here are no shortcuts to peace or to health, yet our modern culture seems to persist in its efforts to find them. There seems to be a "quick-fix" solution for just about everything. Experience tells us that these solutions are rarely satisfying.

Healthy growth and sustainable change are governed by universal natural laws. If we really look, it's easy to see that there's no lasting peace when we try to impose our will on the natural order of things. We can learn this from tending a garden, where ordinary tasks can reveal extraordinary wisdom.

Natural laws don't cut corners. They teach patience and cooperation. In taking care of a garden, we prepare the soil, plant the seeds, protect the seedlings, water, feed, weed, prune, and harvest—each task in its own time. We work with the warmth, light, and water that nature provides and adapt to changing conditions. We anticipate the hour of ripening, and harvest when it arrives. The ripening process follows its own rhythms and not our demands for quick results.

In the garden, timing is everything. We learn to respond to the garden's changing needs, and to respect the cyclic rhythms of growth and ripening, decline and gestation. We become more accepting when we see these same rhythms at work in our personal circumstances. It becomes obvious that, in the long run, skipping steps doesn't work. Neither does trying to harvest something before it's ripe.

The seeds of genuine peace are scattered everywhere. With care, they too will grow by natural laws, and growth and ripening will take their due course. Today's theme focuses on cultivating peace by working in harmony with these laws.

As gardeners, we look to see what's needed. We take the action that makes sense in the natural order of things. A fruitful, healthy harvest is the result of consistent care in the garden, and in daily life. Peace grows as we tend the seeds with patience and common sense. Today you might ask:

Where are the seeds of peace in my life?
What is the natural next step I can take to help them grow?

The *rhythm of peace* also grows by natural laws. In this harmony lies its potential to persist and thrive through seasons of challenge and change. Together we will sow the seeds of peace, and use the wisdom of natural laws to feed and water with care.

day 20 ~ *Natural Laws*

The older I grow,
the more I trust in the law
by which the Rose and the Lily bloom.

JOHANN WOLFGANG VON GOETHE

~

Whoever loves and understands a garden
will find contentment that lasts a lifetime.

CHINESE PROVERB

~

The invariable mark of wisdom
is to see the miraculous in the common.

RALPH WALDO EMERSON

day 20 ~ *Natural Laws*

_____

_____

_____

_____

_____

_____

_____

_____

_____

_____

_____

_____

_____

_____

_____

_____

_____

_____

_____

_____

_____

_____

As I was striving to cultivate beauty in my garden,
I realized that my garden was cultivating peace in me.

day 20 ~ *Natural Laws*

_____

_____

_____

_____

_____

_____

_____

_____

_____

_____

_____

_____

_____

_____

_____

_____

*We will live in peace
when the laws of the world
unite with the laws of nature.
Then will our lives reflect
the harmony of the universe.*

ANONYMOUS

day 20 ~ *Natural Laws*

_____

_____

_____

_____

_____

_____

_____

_____

_____

_____

_____

_____

_____

_____

_____

_____

_____

_____

I get optimism from the Earth itself.
I feel that as long as the Earth
can make a spring every year, I can!
ALICE WALKER

21st day of the month

Great Rhythms

Remember the big picture.

day 21 ~ *Great Rhythms*

Remember the big picture.

We each have a path to travel in life and an allotment of time to travel it. The seasons of our lives unfold against the background of the Great Rhythms of the earth and the sun—rhythms that sustain us every day. The twenty-first day of the month naturally draws our attention to these larger rhythms, especially during the months of a season change.

Each season has come before and each will come again. We can depend on this, no matter what changes for us personally or nationally. Unlike many of our human rhythms, which are vulnerable to stress and chaos, the harmony of the Great Rhythms is certain, and with this certainty comes a breath of peace.

As we reflect on the Great Rhythms, we gain perspective. In the presence of their mysterious harmony, we expand. We stand back and lift our gaze from the details in front of us. We look out over the whole panorama of our lives and see the threads that connect where we've been with where we're going. We take the long view.

day 21 ~ Great Rhythms

We're reminded that we're not islands in this sea of life and that whatever today's weather, it will change. In the grand scope of things, our personal challenges take on new meaning, and we're supported in reconnecting with the deeper purposes of life.

Today's theme turns our attention to the larger rhythms of life. It's a day to take note of sunrise and sunset, the mood of nature, the light and colors of the season, and the messages from the stars. In the larger context of our life story we can each ask:

What are the key themes in my life this month?
Am I doing what I need to do?
Is there something that I need to change?

By reflecting on the Great Rhythms, we invite order and perspective into today's challenges. The *rhythm of peace* finds its home in the Great Rhythms that enfold us all.

Amidst the familiar seasonal rhythms,
there weaves the magical, unpredictable element
that makes each moment unique.
Let us not miss the magic in this day.

ANONYMOUS

day 21 ~ Great Rhythms

Each day in the cycle of the year emanates its own
light and color and sound.
Each day has a unique thread
in the fabric of creation.
Each day releases its own fragrance,
a promise that it will return once again,
exactly one year from now,
familiar and yet new.
I find this infinitely reassuring.

ANONYMOUS

~

When the questions are too big,
and the answers are not yet in time,
I look to the sky.
In starlight there are answers
to newer, older unframed questions.
Ancient light, our reassurance,
emitted with or without hope,
to be caught by a loving, skyward eye.

F. LYNNE BACHLEDA

day 21 ~ Great Rhythms

day 21 ~ Great Rhythms

I firmly believe that nature brings solace
in all troubles.

ANNE FRANK

day 21 ~ *Great Rhythms*

_____
_____
_____
_____
_____
_____
_____
_____
_____
_____
_____
_____
_____
_____
_____
_____
_____
_____
_____
_____
_____
_____
_____
_____

Climb the mountains and get their good tidings.
Nature's peace will flow into you as sunshine flows into trees.

JOHN MUIR

22nd day of the month

Peace with the Earth

Respect the earth.

day 22 ~ *Peace with the Earth*

Respect the earth.

The vision of peace on earth *must* include peace with the earth. Acknowledging our deep connection with the earth is today's theme. When human rhythms break down, the impact on the earth is dramatic. Our collective disharmony spreads like an infection throughout the kingdoms of nature, and results in the depletion, pollution, and destruction of life-giving resources for all.

Not so long ago, many people in the Western world viewed the relationship with the earth as one of "used" and "user"—the earth provided abundant resources and human beings were entitled to use them without restraint. To support urban-industrial ways of life and the desire for unlimited growth, many lost sight of a healthy relationship with the earth. Fortunately, this is changing dramatically.

In the last fifty years, millions of people have awakened to the importance of a healthy partnership with the earth. And with this awakening has come a worldwide movement to restore balance between human rhythms and earth rhythms. In 1962 only twenty percent of Americans thought taking care of the environment

was a serious concern. Today, most of us want a healthy relationship with the earth. Awareness of the profound importance of this
relationship continues to grow as we face urgent questions about
the connection between human activities and climate change. A
worldwide dialog about these questions is leading us to a much
deeper understanding of our individual and shared responsibility
for the health of our planet.

The earth has been speaking, and many are listening. Men
and women from across the world are providing inspiration and
facts to educate us about the needs of our living planet. As a
result, many of us now accept the responsibility of caring for the
earth, and strive to do so with a generous heart. Many of us—but
not all. The conflict over the use of the earth's resources rages on,
and the consequences affect everyone.

On each day of each season, in all parts of the world, the
earth is communicating. Today's theme invites us to connect with
the earth—to tread lightly, and to be grateful for what we receive
and awake to what we must protect. This is a matter for the heart
to consider.

If we listen with our hearts, we will know what to do and
how to do it, and this will change the way we live. The use of the

earth's resources will be tempered by respect and compassion, and our collective efforts will gradually restore harmony and embrace the earth in the *rhythm of peace.*[8]

> *Like friends, nature tells you its secrets*
> *only when it knows you care.*
> *Just practice listening with your eyes,*
> *and one day when you least expect it,*
> *you will see with your heart*
> *and be swept up into nature's dance.*
>
> JOHANN WOLFGANG VON GOETHE

~

> *The frog does not drink up*
> *the pond in which he lives.*
>
> INDIAN PROVERB

---

[8] Visit www.rhythmofpeace.org, *Community Center: Live in Peace with the Earth,* for resources that support a healthy relationship with the earth.

day 22 ~ Peace with the Earth

day 22 ~ Peace with the Earth

... speak to the earth,
and it shall teach thee.

JOB 12:8

day 22 ~ *Peace with the Earth*

I will restore the earth where I am,
use no more of its resources than I need,
and listen, listen to what it is telling me.

M. J. SLIM HOOEY

Truth

Stand for the truth.

day 23 ~ *Truth*

Stand for the truth.

*W*e live in an era where lies and deceptions are all around us. In this environment, we're also vulnerable to self-deception. Opinions get treated as facts, and truth is easily veiled in the dense smog of propaganda. Mechanical social responses mask genuine feelings. Stress causes us to *react* with fight or flight before we can *respond* with authenticity. False realities get spun and packaged with frightening speed using the newest technologies. It's so refreshing when someone enlivens a conversation with an honest, direct expression of truth. There's nothing that can clear the air like the truth.

Within our hearts, we each carry the ability to sense whether or not we're in the presence of truth. In common speech we express this ability with phrases like "that rings true to me," or "I can *feel* the truth of it." We may not know why we feel that way, we just *know*.

We can also sense when something we see or hear isn't true. We're all bombarded with information from many sources every day. How much of it is true? So much of what we hear is mechanical and lacks warmth, wisdom, and basic common sense. Ideas that appear exciting or inviting at first glance are often not

day 23 ~ Truth

grounded in the truth at all. These days, when there are many forces trying to seduce us into thinking that *true is false* and *false is true*, our inner compass for truth may get buried in the turmoil.

Today's theme affirms the value of bringing the light of truth into our conversations and decisions. We can focus on the truth. We can look for it, listen for it, strive to speak it, and let it shape our actions. We can use our natural ability to sense its presence or its absence, and be awake to where we might be prone to self-deception.

The challenge is to have the courage to stand for the truth, and refuse to cooperate with what we know in our hearts is not true. As we let the light of truth shine into our activities today, we help to reveal and dissolve the falseness within and around us. We bring fresh insight to our personal challenges and new clarity to the *rhythm of peace*. We can feel confident that the light of truth will guide us down the path to peace.

Speed is not life force;
adrenaline is not life force;
money is not life force.
Only the presence and articulation of truth is life force.
MARIANNE WILLIAMSON

Release us
from the cowardice that shrinks from new truth,
from the laziness that is content with half-truths,
from the arrogance that thinks it knows all truth.

ANONYMOUS

day 23 ~ *Truth*

Our life is a long and arduous quest after Truth.

MAHATMA GANDHI

Simplicity

Make room for peace.

day 24 ~ Simplicity

Make room for peace.

Daily life is complicated. Sometimes it's far more complicated than it needs to be. Our culture is preoccupied with fullness. We live in a part of the world where over-consumption and accumulation continue to be rewarded. This bias distorts a healthy balance in the natural rhythm of emptiness and fullness, and creates the common condition of being "too full." Too full of what? It's easy to name many things. *Food. "Stuff." Stress. Information. Unfinished business. Incomplete tasks. Undigested thoughts and feelings.*

It's a challenge for all of us to find a healthy answer to the question, "How much is *enough?*" It's one of the most urgent questions of our times. Many of us know that in the long run, too much of anything is not satisfying. Clutter and excess dull our senses, waste precious resources, and work against our efforts for peace.

Today's theme offers a reflection on the many benefits of cultivating simplicity. By intentionally exercising restraint in one area of life, we make room for fullness in another. We can find examples of this principle everywhere. When we reduce our intake of food to just what we need, we have more energy.

day 24 ~ *Simplicity*

When we willingly share some of our resources with others, we're filled with the warmth of kinship and service. Clearing our environment of unnecessary clutter reveals the hidden beauty of order and simplicity. Sacrificing quantity often enriches the experience of quality.

Today is an opportunity to lighten our lives of the non-essential, and to pay attention to what we consume. There are many ways to approach a healthy balance of emptiness and fullness. Consider one of these today: *Eat lightly. Reduce excess. Spend carefully. Take only what you need. Avoid fueling mental or emotional turmoil—yours or another's. Choose quality. Reduce toxicity. Eliminate clutter. Conserve energy. Savor simplicity.*

Through our efforts to cultivate simplicity, we make room for peace. We find a renewed appreciation of the fullness we have, rather than taking it for granted. We temper the mindset that more is better. Through practicing the balance of emptiness and fullness, we learn to appreciate genuine sufficiency—not too much and not too little—and contribute a refreshing simplicity to the *rhythm of peace.*

day 24 ~ *Simplicity*

In the search for satisfaction,
millions of people are not only "downshifting"
or pulling back from the rat race,
they are also "upshifting" or moving ahead into a life that is,
though materially more modest,
rich with family, friends, community,
creative work in the world,
and a soulful connection with the universe.

DUANE ELGIN

~

In pursuit of knowledge,
every day something is acquired.
In pursuit of wisdom,
every day something is dropped.

LAO TSU

day 24 ~ *Simplicity*

This frail vessel thou emptiest again and again,
and fillest it ever with fresh life.
This little flute of a reed
thou hast carried over hills and dales,
and has breathed through it melodies
eternally new ...
Thy infinite gifts come to me only on
those very small hands of mine.
Ages pass, and still thou pourest,
and still there is room to fill.

RABINDRANATH TAGORE

~

Where there is too much,
something is missing.

JEWISH PROVERB

day 24 ~ *Simplicity*

New seed is faithful.
It roots deepest in the places
that are most empty.

CLARISSA PINKOLA ESTÉS

day 24 ~ *Simplicity*

The ability to simplify
means to eliminate the unnecessary
so that the necessary may speak.

HANS HOFMANN

May the spirit of peace
live in the hearts of all people.

Welcome the spirit of peace.

day 25 ~ *Spirit*

Welcome the spirit of peace.

At this very moment, the spirit of peace is awakening and inspiring human hearts throughout the world. This universal spirit moves us to express our good will to each other in ways that transcend gender, class, race, religion, and nationality. It guides us in recognizing our common humanity, and helps us to embrace our differences.

Though the spirit of peace resides in every human heart, it's up to each one of us to recognize it, awaken it, and give it expression. When we do, we can begin to see its healing influence in every aspect of life. Today's theme is an invitation to be receptive to the spirit of peace.

There are many opportunities for receiving gifts of peace and good will in life. Our receptivity to these blessings is a factor in how they impact us. Sometimes a blessing touches us in a meaningful way. On those occasions we may feel it as a soothing breeze that uplifts and refreshes—a tangible presence of peace. At other times, a blessing that is intended for us passes by unnoticed because we have neither the time nor the space to receive it.

day 25 ~ *Spirit*

Receiving is an art in its own right. We prepare for it by
reducing excess, as we did yesterday. We exercise our abilities
to yield, open, and allow. We pause in our doing and achieving,
shift our attention from the busyness of life, and listen to what is
calling to us from deep within our own hearts.

Let's be receptive to the spirit of peace today, and stay alert
to the many ways it might influence our thoughts, feelings,
and actions. It might be through an inspiration to take action
or through a deep calmness in the face of a challenge. It might
be through a desire to end a cold war with a family member or
friend. Maybe we will find the strength we need to say "no" to
an inner or outer tyrant. Or maybe we will interact with
someone today who unexpectedly awakens us and softens our
heart. We might be reminded that the heart speaks all languages.

As we join together to welcome the spirit of peace, we can
imagine it touching receptive hearts everywhere—healing
isolation, illuminating darkness, inspiring actions—and nourishing
opportunities for peace and justice throughout the world. *May
we each be touched today by the spirit of peace*, may it move us to
meaningful action, and may it bring new light and warmth to the
rhythm of peace.

day 25 ~ *Spirit*

The first peace,
which is the most important,
is that which comes within the souls of people
when they realize their relationship,
their oneness with the universe and all its powers,
and when they realize that
at the center of the universe dwells the Great Spirit,
and that this center is really everywhere,
it is within each of us.

BLACK ELK

~

In the hearts of people today
there is a deep longing for peace.
When the true spirit of peace is thoroughly dominant,
it becomes an inner experience
with unlimited possibilities.
Only when this really happens—
when the spirit of peace awakens
and takes possession of human hearts,
can humanity be saved from perishing.

ALBERT SCHWEITZER

day 25 ~ *Spirit*

day 25 ~ *Spirit*

day 25 ~ *Spirit*

No peace lies in the future which is not hidden
in this present instant.
Seek peace!

FRA GIOVANNI

Poetry

Renew your imagination.

day 26 ~ *Poetry*

Renew your imagination.

Good poetry refreshes the imagination and offers a healthy break from daily tensions, opening us to new or forgotten possibilities. The creative use of the word captures an essence that releases its sustenance to a receiving heart. Poetry offers color—sometimes intense color—for which the imagination so hungers when life becomes too familiar or too chaotic, and all we see are dull tones. When poetry strikes a chord in us, it reflects back both the heights and the depths of our human experience and we feel "seen."

Through writing poetry we claim our voice as we engage in a direct conversation with life. We grapple with the realities before us and strive to sculpt a sense of meaning. In reading a piece of poetry that moves us, we enter into the world of art, beauty, and depth. We become more attuned to the full impact of the present moment.

The poetry of peace provides an important source of nourishment for the sustained effort that cultivating peace requires. Today's theme recommends taking a few minutes to renew your imagination by reading or writing some poetry for peace. Be soothed or startled, inspired or humbled … whatever you need today.

If possible, share some poetry you love with your family, friends or co-workers. As we engage our imagination today, by letting ourselves be influenced by the creative power of the word, we bring new inspiration to the *rhythm of peace*.[9]

The Lightest Touch

Good poetry begins with
the lightest touch,
a breeze arriving from nowhere,
a whispered healing arrival,
a word in your ear,
a settling into things,
then like a hand in the dark
it arrests the whole body,
steeling you for revelation.

…

DAVID WHYTE

---

[9] Visit www.rhythmofpeace.org, *Community Center: Read the Poetry of Peace*, to read poetry submitted by members of the *rhythm of peace* community.

Peace and Eggshells

Peace is a dove carrying a laurel branch
Peace is a loving gesture
Peace is hands joined around the planet
Peace is a Pilgrim
Peace is a prayer by St. Francis
Peace is two friends feasting their eyes on each other
Peace is a tranquil dwelling within
Peace has a rhythm
Time was when I thought that peace
was something you kept
until I found that in keeping the peace,
I gave myself away.
Walking on eggshells is no peace at all,
is at least a hollow and fleeting peace
exacting too high a price
and besides, quite messy underfoot!
Peace is a choice
...

BARBARA SUTER

day 26 ~ Poetry

day 26 ~ Poetry

day 26 ~ Poetry

No coward soul is mine,
No trembler in the world's storm-troubled sphere:
I see Heaven's glories shine,
And faith shines equal, arming me from fear.

EMILY BRONTE

He who cannot forgive
breaks the bridge
over which he himself must pass.

GEORGE HERBERT

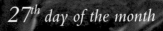
27th day of the month

27

Forgiveness

Forgive someone today.

day 27 ~ *Forgiveness*

Forgive someone today.

It is an unavoidable fact of relationship that people often don't act the way we think they should. How we handle this is one of life's greatest challenges.

Everyone needs forgiveness. The darker side of human nature is everyone's challenge. We make mistakes and errors every day. In our relationships, we struggle with one another. We can be cruel. In every aspect of human life we can easily find examples of one person's will stubbornly braced against another's. Sometimes the conflict seems endless, as does the suffering that accompanies it.

We each need something that lifts the weight of our own and each other's accumulated mistakes. We need to be able to start again—to learn, correct, make amends, understand, heal, and move on. Genuine forgiveness offers this while *never* condoning cruelty or injustice.

Many of the world's wisdom traditions recognize forgiveness as a spiritual practice that can bring peace to the soul. Recent research has demonstrated that forgiveness is also good for physical and emotional health as it reduces stress on the body and especially the heart. Old resentments that become inflamed every time we think about them can wage a brutal war with health as well as with peace.

With every resentment and grudge, every loss and betrayal, there is a right time to make peace. Today's theme suggests that we review our memories for a recent or long-standing resentment or grievance that we might be willing to release. *Is there one that comes to mind?*

Forgiveness is an active process. It must be freely chosen, not forced. We choose it among the many ways we might respond to hurt or injustice. We choose the timing. In the empty space created by releasing resentment, the spirit of peace and healing can enter.[10]

It might not be easy to make the choice to forgive, but it may be time. May our reflections on forgiveness today reduce suffering, restore hope, and bring a stream of true justice into the *rhythm of peace.*

---

[10] Visit www.rhythmofpeace.org, *Community Center: Communicate for Peace*, for resources on forgiveness.

day 27 ~ *Forgiveness*

_____

_____

_____

_____

_____

_____

_____

_____

_____

_____

_____

_____

_____

_____

_____

_____

_____

_____

_____

Without forgiveness there is no future.
To forgive is the only way to
permanently change the world.
ARCHBISHOP DESMOND TUTU

day 27 ~ *Forgiveness*

*You will know that forgiveness has begun
when you recall those who hurt you
and feel the power to wish them well.*

LEWIS B. SMEDES

Bless our souls
as our bodies sleep
so we may hear
the melodies of peace.

J. RAE

Rest

Enjoy the peace of the night.

day 28 ~ *Rest*

Enjoy the peace of the night.

Everyone knows that productivity, creativity, and well-being are enriched when we're well rested. But getting a deep and refreshing sleep is not as easy as it used to be. It's frustrating to stay awake, tossing and turning with a restless mind, when we want and need to sleep. Many describe the familiar experience of watching the clock, worrying about losing sleep, thinking about the looming pressure of the next day's activities, and finding it more and more difficult to relax.

A good night's sleep comes from a balance in the rhythm of rest and activity. It's so common to have *too little* deep rest and *too much* restless activity. Sometimes, the day is just too fast, too intense or too busy to unwind and relax naturally when it's time to sleep. This is a symptom of the gap between the slower rhythms of our bodies and the faster speeds of technology-based lifestyles that we're used to during our waking hours.

There's nothing that compares to the peace of the night—moonlight, starlight, firelight, candlelight—a natural time for reflection, deep rest, and renewal for body and soul. There's a naturally fertile time—after we finish the day's activities and

day 28 ~ Rest

before we fall asleep—that's especially suited to peace. But often this time is filled with weariness and depletion or the last-minute tasks of the day.

This time doesn't need to be sacrificed to fatigue. It can be a time for reviewing the day, welcoming the creative impulses that gestate in the darkness, and choosing carefully the thoughts, images, and questions we take with us into sleep. It's a time to savor and enjoy just how healing it is to slow down and take a long, slow exhale. When we take a few minutes to prepare for sleep, we find new reserves of energy in the night. And then tomorrow's activities will be enriched by that special wisdom that only comes to us from a deep and peaceful sleep.

A suggestion for tonight: During the last half hour before you go to sleep, take a few minutes to review your day. Take special note of the moments for which you have gratitude, and clarify the most important questions and concerns you have in your life right now. Take these questions with you into the night, and anticipate the guidance you may receive in the morning when you awake.

If we believe life is fundamentally good,
we will seek out rest as a taste of that goodness.
WAYNE MULLER

day 28 ~ Rest

Our lack of rest and reflection is not just a personal affliction.
It colors the way we build and sustain community,
it dictates the way we respond to suffering, and it
shapes the ways in which we seek peace and healing in the world.

WAYNE MULLER

day 28 ~ *Rest*

Take rest;
a field that has rested gives a bountiful crop.

OVID

29th day of the month

29

Community

Celebrate the gifts of community.

day 29 ~ *Community*

Celebrate the gifts of community.

A sense of belonging and a meaningful connection to other people are basic human needs. Everyone deserves the warmth and support of a community of people who share values, interests, and concerns. Our close ties to one another help buffer the hardships in life and encourage the victories. Today's theme celebrates community and acknowledges the importance of our networks of support.

Where in your life do you feel valued, understood, and appreciated? Who are the people you count on for good companionship, honest communication, and empathy?

When we're isolated, our efforts may seem insignificant and our impact small. But when we work together, we see the results of shared intention, partnership, and synergy. As we combine support and appreciation for each other with a common purpose— such as cultivating peace—we create a healthy community that is both enriching personally and powerful in its capacity to bring about change. Today we honor both our personal support networks as well as the larger community of peace-minded people around the world of which we are a part.

day 29 ~ *Community*

The pulse of the global network for peace is tangible. It beats steadily beneath the noise and intensity of daily life. If we connect with it, we can feel the hum of possibility and vitality as it tirelessly penetrates the darkness of the world. Those of us participating in the *Rhythm of Peace* Project contribute to this pulse each day, as do many, many others. Let's celebrate all the efforts made this month from around the world to call forth a peaceful future.

We will continue to care, to commit, to work, to overcome, to pray, to celebrate, to believe, and to dream. We will each do this in our own ways, and we will do it together. Today we affirm that our shared commitment to peace is a potent force for healing in the world.

We recognize the millions of individual contributions and the value of each one. We extend to those who feel isolated and alone. We welcome the sustenance that community offers. *Connection, meaning, encouragement, warmth*—these are some of the gifts of community. In celebrating community, we feel the hope of our combined efforts to bring about lasting peace in our hearts and homes, and in the world.

A suggestion for today: This is a good day to actively participate in expanding the grassroots network for peace by

day 29 ~ Community

inviting someone you know to join the next cycle of the *rhythm of peace* that begins on the first of the month. Every person's unique contribution enriches the community for us all.[11]

Healthy social life is only found
when in the mirror of each human soul
the whole community forms its reflection,
and when in the community
the strength of each individual is living.

RUDOLF STEINER

~

To know someone here and there
who thinks and feels with us,
and though distant is close to us in spirit,
this makes the earth for us
an inhabited garden.

JOHANN WOLFGANG VON GOETHE

---

[11] Visit www.rhythmofpeace.org, *Tell a Friend*, to invite your friends, co-workers, and family members to participate in making peace a daily priority. Also, visit the *Community Center: Get Together with Friends*, for suggestions on meeting in small groups to support actions that cultivate peace in daily life.

day 29 ~ *Community*

day 29 ~ *Community*

day 29 ~ *Community*

We were born to come together for a purpose.
Recognizing this makes all the difference.

Completion

Practice the art of letting go.

days 30 & 31 ~ *Completion*

Practice the art of letting go.

*T*oday completes this month's cycle of the *rhythm of peace*. It's an ending, and endings invite us to pause, look back, and reflect. You might ask:

What has happened in my life this month?
What has happened in the world?

As we recall the highlights of the month, and revisit them briefly in our memory, we practice the art of letting go. As with any ability, it becomes more seasoned and graceful with time. Some of the events of this month may stay with us for awhile. We'll let go gradually as time passes, as we come to terms with what we've experienced. Wisdom tells us what to leave behind and what to carry with us into the new month.

A review of the month helps us to digest and assimilate our experiences. The consequences of our actions and choices are easier to see. We notice what worked and what didn't. We remember those circumstances that moved and inspired, as well as those that disappointed and frustrated. We embrace crisis or hardship with compassion, and acknowledge turning points.

days 30 & 31 ~ *Completion*

As we look back, we find some things to correct, and other things to acknowledge and celebrate. We see some of the results of our efforts to cultivate peace. If we discover we're still lingering in past events, our intention to let go helps restore us to the present moment. Maybe we're reminded of something unfinished that can be completed today.

An end-of-the-month review supports health because it releases tension and prevents an unnecessary build-up of unfinished business. Reflection supports peace because it fosters stillness and acceptance. We gain perspective on how we're living, and see the twists and turns of our destiny through the passage of time. When we've done what we can, then we let go, exhale fully, and carry the wisdom of this month's living forward.

> *Finish each day and be done with it.*
> *You have done what you could.*
> *Some blunders and absurdities no doubt crept in;*
> *let go of them as soon as you can.*
> *Tomorrow is a new day;*
> *you shall begin it well and serenely.*
> RALPH WALDO EMERSON

days 30 & 31 ~ *Completion*

days 30 & 31 ~ *Completion*

If thou hast commenced a good action,
leave it not incomplete.

THE TALMUD

days 30 & 31 ~ Completion

days 30 & 31 ~ Completion

Thank you
for participating
in the *rhythm of peace* this month!

The next cycle begins
on the first of the month
as we continue to make peace a daily priority...

~

History shows that even seemingly miraculous advances
are in fact the result of
many people taking small steps together
over a long period of time.
PAUL LOEB

Permissions

We gratefully acknowledge the individuals and publishers who granted us permission to use their copyrighted material. A thorough effort has been made to locate all rights holders. To the best of our knowledge, all quotes in this book not sited below fall under the fair use and public domain guidelines of copyright law in the United States of America. If any acknowledgments have been omitted or errors made, please notify us so we can make necessary corrections before the next printing.

PHOTOGRAPHS

Hodges, Randall J. Photographs for cover and themes 12, 17, 18, and 27 by Randall J. Hodges, copyright Randall J. Hodges Photography, www.randalljhodges.com. Used with permission from the photographer.

Lavender, Laurent. Photograph for theme 15 by Laurent Lavender, www.pixheaven.net. Used with permission from the photographer.

M.C. Commercial Photography. Photograph for theme 19 by Michael Chafran, copyright © 2008, mcphoto1@msn.com. Used with permission from the photographer.

All other images used in this book are royalty-free images purchased as individual images or image collections from Getty Images, www.gettyimages.com.

TEXT

Bachleda, F. Lynne, *Blue Mountain: A Spiritual Anthology Celebrating the Earth*, copyright © 2000 by F. Lynne Bachleda, page 18. Used with permission from Menasha Ridge Press, Birmingham, AL. (theme 21)

Bryant, William, *The Veiled Pulse of Time*, pages 14 and 28, copyright © 1993, Lindisfarne Books. Used with permission. (themes 7 and 15)

Campbell, Joseph, *The Power of Myth*, page 217, by Joseph Campbell and Bill Moyers, copyright © 1988 by Apostrophe S Productions, Inc. and Bill Moyers and Alfred Van der Marck Editions, Inc. for itself and the estate of Joseph Campbell. Used with permission from Doubleday, a division of Random House, Inc. (theme 14)

Carroll, James. Used with permission from the author. (theme 14)

Chödrön, Pema, *Practicing Peace in Times of War*, copyright © 2006. Reprinted by arrangement with Shambhala Publications Inc., Boston, MA, www.shambhala.com. (theme 12)

Covey, Stephen, *First Things First*, page 291. (theme 13)
The 7 Habits of Highly Effective People, page 239. (theme 16)
Used with permission from the author, www.stephencovey.com.

Elgin, Duane, *Promise Ahead: A Vision of Hope and Action for Humanity's Future*, pages 13 and 68. (themes 11 and 14)
"The Garden of Simplicity," page 2, *Emerging Lifestyles* magazine, Spring, 2003. (theme 24) Used with permission from the author.

Estés, Clarissa Pinkola. "New Seed" prayer by Clarissa Pinkola Estés, Ph.D. from *The Faithful Gardener*, Harper San Francisco, copyright © 1995, 2007, C.P. Estés. Reprinted with kind permission from the publisher and author. (theme 24)

Graham, Martha. Permission given by the Estate of Martha Graham, c/o Ronald Protas and the Seraphic Dialogue Theatre and Dance Foundation. (theme 3)

Harmon, Willis. New Dimensions' program #2992, "Peace is a Verb," www.newdimensions.org. Used with permission. (theme 5)

His Holiness the Dalai Lama. Permission granted by The Office of Tibet in New York, New York. (theme 2)

Hooey, M.J. Slim. Quoted from www.gardendigest.com. Used with permission. (theme 22)

Keller, Helen. Courtesy of the American Foundation for the Blind, Helen Keller Archives. (themes 5 and 8)

Loeb, Paul, *The Impossible Will Take a Little While: A Citizen's Guide to Hope in a Time of Fear*. Used with permission from the author. (theme 30/31)

Macy, Joanna, *Prayers for a Thousand Years*, edited by Elizabeth Roberts and Elias Amidon, page 158. Used with permission from the author. (theme 11)

Merton, Thomas, *No Man Is an Island*, Harvest/HBJ Book, 2002, page 127. (theme 15)
The Hidden Ground of Love, the letters of Thomas Merton on religious experience and social concerns, selected and edited by William H. Shannon, New York: Farrar, Straus, Giroux, 1985, page 116. The quote appears in a letter from Thomas Merton to Amiya Chakravarty on April 13, 1967. (theme 19)

Muller, Wayne, *Sabbath: Restoring the Sacred Rhythm of Rest*, pages 3, 11, 40, and 43, Bantam Books, 1999. Used with permission from the author. (themes 7, 14, 18, and 28)

Norris, Gunilla, *Inviting Silence*, page 8, published by BlueBridge, New York. Used with permission. (theme 19)

Parks, Rosa. Permission granted by the Rosa and Raymond Parks Institute for Self-Development. (theme 11)

Pathways to Peace. Permission granted by Pathways to Peace, www.pathwaystopeace.org. (theme 1)

Peace Pilgrim. Permission to use given by Friends of Peace Pilgrim, a 501(c)(3) non-profit California corporation. Office, library, retreat center, and archives are located at Friends of Peace Pilgrim, 4399 Buckboard Drive, Box 423, Copperopolis, CA, 95228. (theme 3)

Powell, Robert. This verse by Rudolf Steiner was translated into English by Robert Powell for Choreocosmos workshops (see Lacquanna Paul & Robert Powell, *Cosmic Dances of the Zodiac*, Sophia Foundation Press, San Rafael, California, 2007). Used with permission of the translator. (theme 17)

Rae, J. Conversation with the author. Used with permission. (theme 28)

Roerich, Nicholas. Permission granted by Pathways to Peace, www.pathwaystopeace.org. (dedication page)

Smedes, Lewis B., *Forgive and Forget*, copyright © 1984 by Lewis B. Smedes. Reprinted by permission from HarperCollins Publishers. (theme 27)

Spangler, David, *Blessing: The Art and the Practice*, pages 4 and 23. Used with permission from the author. (theme 18)

Steiner, Rudolf. November, 1920. Listed in *Verses and Meditations* from Steiner Books, www.steinerbooks.org. Used with permission from the American Association of Waldorf Schools. (theme 29)

Straub, Gail, *The Rhythm of Compassion: Caring for Self, Connecting with Society*, inside jacket. Used with permission from the author. (theme 10)

Suter, Barbara, *Peace and Eggshells*. Used with permission from the author. (theme 26)

Thich Nhat Hanh. Permission to use given by Plum Village Meditation Center with locations at: Deer Park Monastery in Escondido, California; Maple Forest Monastery and Green Mt. Dharma Center in Vermont; and the main Meditation Center in Southern France. They can be reached at www.plumvillage.org. (theme 2)

Thoele, Sue Patton. Excerpted from the *Woman's Book of Soul* by Sue Patton Thoele, copyright © 1997, 1998 with permission of Conari Press, imprint of Red Wheel/Weiser, Newburyport, MA and San Francisco, CA, www.redwheelweiser.com. (theme 16)

Tutu, Archbishop Desmond, *No Future without Forgiveness*, Doubleday, 1999. Used with permission. (theme 27)

Walker, Alice. New Dimensions' program #2963-64, "Activism with Heart and Soul: A Dialogue with Alice Walker," www.newdimensions.org. Used with permission. (theme 20)

Resources

Alliance for a New Humanity
www.anhglobal.org

Bachleda, F. Lynne
Blue Mountain: A Spiritual Anthology Celebrating the Earth

Bryant, William
The Veiled Pulse of Time: Life Cycles and Destiny

Childre, Doc and Rozman, Deborah
Transforming Stress: The Heartmath Solution for Relieving Worry, Fatigue, and Tension
www.heartmath.com

Chödrön, Pema
Practicing Peace in Times of War
www.pemachodron.org

Chopra, Deepak
Peace is the Way
www.chopra.com
www.onlinepeacecell.com

Covey, Stephen R.
First Things First
The 7 Habits of Highly Effective People
www.stephencovey.com

Covey, Stephen M. R.
The Speed of Trust
www.speedoftrust.com

Elgin, Duane
Promise Ahead: A Vision of Hope and Action for Humanity's Future
www.awakeningearth.org

Estés, Clarissa Pinkola, Ph.D.
The Creative Fire (audio tape)

Gore, Al
An Inconvenient Truth
www.algore.com

His Holiness the Dalai Lama
Ethics for the New Millennium
www.dalailama.com

Karren, Hafen, Smith, and Frandsen
Mind/Body Health: The Effects of Attitudes, Emotions, and Relationships

Loeb, Paul
Soul of a Citizen
The Impossible Will Take a Little While
www.paulloeb.org

Luskin, Fred, Ph.D.
Forgive for Good
www.learningtoforgive.com

Muller, Wayne
Sabbath: Restoring the Sacred Rhythm of Rest
www.breadforthejourney.org

New Dimensions Foundation
www.newdimensions.org

Pathways to Peace
www.pathwaystopeace.org

Ray, Paul and Anderson, Sherry Ruth
The Cultural Creatives: How 50 Million People are Changing the World
www.culturalcreatives.org

Roberts, Elizabeth, Ed.D. and Amidon, Elias
Prayers for a Thousand Years
www.boulderinstitute.org

Rosenberg, Marshall, Ph.D.
Nonviolent Communication: A Language of Life
www.cnvc.org

Rossi, Ernest Lawrence, Ph.D.
The 20 Minute Break: Using the New Science of Ultradian Rhythms
www.ernestrossi.com

Spangler, David
Blessing: The Art and the Practice

Steiner, Rudolf
The Cycle of the Year
www.steinerbooks.org

Straub, Gail
The Rhythm of Compassion: Caring for Self, Connecting with Society
www.empowermenttraining.com

The Alliance for Climate Protection
www.wecansolveit.org

The Peace Alliance
www.thepeacealliance.org

Thich Nhat Hanh
Being Peace
www.plumvillage.org

Tutu, Archbishop Desmond
No Future Without Forgiveness
www.tutufoundation-usa.org

Vennard, Jane E.
Embracing the World: Praying for Justice and Peace

Williamson, Marianne
Healing the Soul of America
www.marianne.com

Whyte, David
Crossing the Unknown Sea: Work as a Pilgrimage of Identity
Everything is Waiting for You
www.davidwhyte.com

... anonymous author
Meditations on the Tarot
Translated from French by Robert Powell, Ph.D.
www.sophiafoundation.org

The **Northwest Center for Health Promotion** (NCHP) was founded in 1994 with the mission to educate and inspire people of all ages to live healthy lives and to reduce the health hazards of chronic stress. Its programs emphasize the importance of attending to the complete range of human needs—physical, emotional, mental, social, and spiritual. NCHP affirms the critical link between individual health and social health. It promotes the common sense principle that healthy people make healthier choices, and healthier choices contribute to a more just and humane world. The *Rhythm of Peace* Project is NCHP's newest program and promotes healthy living as a foundation for peace.

Deborah Aikens, Ph.D., is a psychologist with a background in Transpersonal Psychology and behavioral medicine. She has developed and facilitated stress reduction and renewal programs for individuals, groups, and organizations for twenty-five years. She is dedicated to facilitating group and community processes that support personal and social transformation. Currently, Deborah is the director of the Northwest Center for Health Promotion in Eugene, Oregon, and is facilitating the growth and development of the *Rhythm of Peace* Project.

Contact Information & Book Orders

Rhythm of Peace is a project of the **Northwest Center for Health Promotion**, a non-profit educational organization in Eugene, Oregon, USA.

Northwest Center for Health Promotion
90 East 27th Avenue, Suite A
Eugene, OR 97405
541-343-0536
877-343-0536
www.rhythmofpeace.org

Telephone orders: Call 877-343-0536 toll free.

Online orders: Visit the "Store" at www.rhythmofpeace.org. All profits from the sales of the *Rhythm of Peace* book through this website and through activities of the Northwest Center for Health Promotion will be used to educate and inspire people of all ages to make peace a priority in their homes, families, and workplaces.

Donations: Your tax-deductible contributions to the *Rhythm of Peace* Project provide necessary resources to support and expand the diverse community of peace-minded people who strive to cultivate peace and reduce stress in their daily activities. Your participation in this vital grassroots activity is sincerely appreciated. Visit "Donations" at www.rhythmofpeace.org.

E-mail: info@rhythmofpeace.org.